Are You an
Earth
Angel?

About the Author

Tanya Carroll Richardson is a self-improvement/spiritual author, professional intuitive, and regular contributor to MindBody Green.com. Her other books include *Angel Insights*, *Zen Teen*, *Angel Intuition,* and *Forever in My Heart: A Grief Journal.* Sign up for Tanya's free newsletter or follow her on social media by visiting tanyablessings.com.

To Write to the Author

If you wish to contact the author or would like more information about this book, please write to the author in care of Llewellyn Worldwide Ltd. and we will forward your request. Both the author and publisher appreciate hearing from you and learning of your enjoyment of this book and how it has helped you. Llewellyn Worldwide Ltd. cannot guarantee that every letter written to the author can be answered, but all will be forwarded. Please write to:

Tanya Carroll Richardson
⁒ Llewellyn Worldwide
2143 Wooddale Drive
Woodbury, MN 55125-2989
Please enclose a self-addressed stamped envelope for reply,
or $1.00 to cover costs. If outside the U.S.A., enclose
an international postal reply coupon.

Many of Llewellyn's authors have websites with additional information and resources. For more information, please visit our website at http://www.llewellyn.com.

Tanya Carroll Richardson

Understand Your Sensitive & Empathic
Nature & Live with Divine Purpose

Are You an Earth Angel?

Llewellyn Publications
Woodbury, Minnesota

First Edition, first Printing, 2020

Book design: Samantha Penn
Cover design: Kevin R. Brown

Llewellyn Publications is a registered trademark of Llewellyn Worldwide Ltd.

Library of Congress Cataloging-in-Publication Data
Names: Richardson, Tanya Carroll, author.
Title: Are you an earth angel? : understand your sensitive & empathic
   nature & live with divine purpose / Tanya Carroll Richardson.
Description: First edition. | Woodbury, Minnesota : Llewellyn Publications,
   2020. | Summary: "Ways to protect, understand, and make use of your
   sensitivity if you are an Earth Angel, or sensitive person. Includes
   self-care tips and exercises"— Provided by publisher.
Identifiers: LCCN 2020009052 (print) | LCCN 2020009053 (ebook) | ISBN
   9780738762920 (paperback) | ISBN 9780738763231 (ebook)
Subjects: LCSH: Psychics. | Parapsychology.
Classification: LCC BF1040 .R53 2020 (print) | LCC BF1040 (ebook) | DDC
   133.8—dc23
LC record available at https://lccn.loc.gov/2020009052
LC ebook record available at https://lccn.loc.gov/2020009053

Llewellyn Worldwide Ltd. does not participate in, endorse, or have any authority or responsibility concerning private business transactions between our authors and the public.
   All mail addressed to the author is forwarded but the publisher cannot, unless specifically instructed by the author, give out an address or phone number.
   Any internet references contained in this work are current at publication time, but the publisher cannot guarantee that a specific location will continue to be maintained. Please refer to the publisher's website for links to authors' websites and other sources.

Llewellyn Publications
A Division of Llewellyn Worldwide Ltd.
2143 Wooddale Drive
Woodbury, MN 55125-2989
www.llewellyn.com

Printed in the United States of America

Other Books by Tanya Carroll Richardson

Angel Intuition: A Psychic's Guide to the Language of Angels (Llewellyn Publications, 2018)

Angel Insights: Inspiring Messages From and Ways to Connect with Your Spiritual Guardians (Llewellyn Publications, 2016)

Forever in My Heart: A Grief Journal (Ulysses Press, 2016)

Zen Teen: 40 Ways to Stay Calm When Life Gets Stressful (Seal Press/Hachette, 2018)

Heaven on Earth: A Guided Journal for Creating Your Own Divine Paradise (Sterling, 2015)

Self-Care for Empaths: 100 Activities to Help You Relax, Recharge, and Rebalance Your Life (Simon & Schuster, 2020)

Disclaimer

Readers are advised to consult their doctors or other qualified healthcare professionals regarding the treatment of their medical or psychological concerns. Please note that the information in this book is not meant to diagnose, treat, prescribe, or substitute consultation with a licensed healthcare professional.

Contents

Earth Angel Exercise List

Introduction

I told someone I thought she was an earth angel once, and she replied, "I've been called a highly sensitive person and an empath. Please don't give me a new diagnosis!" We both laughed, but I understood her point. I'm guessing that if you picked up this book, you already identify as a highly sensitive person, an empath, or an earth angel. If you aren't familiar with those terms, you will be as we journey together in this book. For now, just trust that your own intuition or inner knowing led you to pick up this title for an important reason.

Sensitivity is something I often explain to clients who come to me for intuitive readings. It's natural that sensitive people would be attracted to working with me, a professional intuitive who relies on her own sensitivity. The majority of my clients are highly sensitive and often empathic as well—I attract many earth angels too. Any clients mentioned in this book have had their names and other details altered to protect their privacy.

Some clients come to me well read or knowledgeable about sensitivity, others know a bit about the topic, and some are being introduced to the concept for the first time (even though they have been sensitive their whole lives and never realized it). Many clients teach me about sensitivity simply by sharing their stories of being a sensitive person out in the world and how sensitivity affects them individually. Sensitivity also happens to be the cardinal trait of earth angels.

The collective earth angel destiny—to guide, inspire, and uplift others—affects every individual earth angel's personal life and destiny. In this book we'll certainly cover earth angels' special sensitivity and how you can take better care of yourself as an earth angel to protect and maximize that sensitivity. Being an earth angel sets you up for some amazingly rich experiences in life, but it also sets you up for encountering some serious potholes—knowing what to expect will help you navigate around them. Earth angels very much value their relationships to others, so we'll talk about how to make the most of your romantic, career, friendship, familial, and even casual relationships.

Besides being a professional intuitive who gives readings to clients all over the world, I'm also an angel enthusiast who has been working with heavenly angels for more than fifteen years. After working with divine angels in sessions with people from all walks of life, the earth angel pattern or archetype began to emerge. I also realized that I myself identify as an earth angel. While I was working on this book, I had several experiences and encounters that forced me to look more closely and seriously at what being an earth angel means: the responsibility but also the deep, beautiful purpose and meaning that comes with it. I hope you find what I've discovered about the earth angel archetype and tried to impart in this book inspiring for your own journey. Being an earth angel is an invitation to see your life more symbolically and to realize that every interaction you have with another person has the possibility to be significant.

The information in this book isn't meant to make you feel fragile, out of place, or as my friend's comment implied, burdened. Sensitivity is a gift and a strength. The more you journey through life with heightened sensitivity, honor it, and learn about it, the more obvious that will become. Unfortunately, identifying as highly sensitive or empathic—earth angels are both—can give some people the impression that they need to hide from or shut out the world. While highly sensitive and empathic people do need retreat time because their sensitive nervous and energetic systems pick up on so much, they don't need to isolate or fear that the world is too much for them. In the case of earth angels, your sensitivities are there to help you help others, something that very much involves you being out in the world.

I hope the information in this book helps you better know yourself, make better decisions, and live with more joy, meaning, and purpose. If a certain chapter or section calls to you strongly as you flip through the book, don't be shy about beginning there. But to really learn all you can about sensitivity, earth angels, and *yourself*, you should read the whole book. Earth angels have a tendency to give a lot to and be very concerned about others. Consider reading this book an important investment in yourself. I hope that when you finish, you look at this book as an owner's manual for the magnificent machine that is you. If you ever need a quick dose of earth angel wisdom or medicine, simply hold the book between your palms (you have two strong chakras located there) for a few seconds and ask your divine angels for a message you need to hear right now. Then open the book at random (you might find it opens for you toward the beginning, middle, or end) and begin reading the information on that page.

After writing two books about celestial angels, I'll be drawing on my work with divine angels often for this book about human earth angels, because earth angels and celestial angels have much in common. Perhaps you enjoy learning about and connecting with divine angels and were curious about *earth* angels, which was why you picked up this book. Some people, like earth angels, do feel a stronger bond with divine angels.

For people who are exceptionally sensitive—to subtle stimuli, the emotions and energy of others—they might have always known they are different. But when someone gives you a roadmap and ground rules, and lets you know you aren't the only one, it can be life changing. My wish is that this book is that nourishing and expansive for you.

As you read along, you may think, "I'm actually *not* an earth angel." You might instead find yourself having the name or face of a loved one, friend, or old teacher or colleague cross your mind. Not everyone is an earth angel, or meant to be. But you have surely had some earth angels cross your path, and this book will help you better understand these people and recognize them. This book may also help you align to earth angel energy. So if you read a section and think, "Yes, please, I'd like more of that in my life," know that earth angel energy is available to all of us.

Consider this book an invitation to connect with your inner earth angel. We all have a little bit of the earth angel inside. It's the impulse to be kind, generous, or merciful to someone else, and then the wonderful feelings of satisfaction, purpose, and warmth you experience afterward.

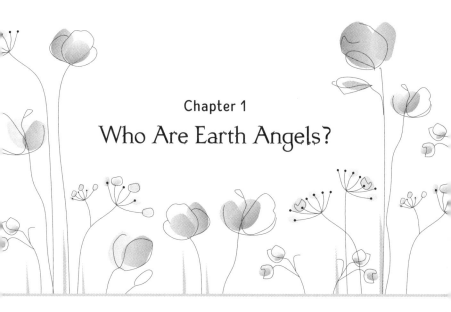

Chapter 1
Who Are Earth Angels?

The term *earth angel* is so simple yet so appropriate and descriptive. The word *earth* reminds us all of something crucial—if you are reading this book, you have incarnated on the earth plane, just like me. As much as we like to talk about the dimension known as heaven and riff about what happens to our souls after we leave this earthly body, it's essential we stay grounded here on earth. This life is what our souls are doing right now, and whether you are going through a challenging time in your life, a joyful phase, or a plateau period, your life needs and deserves your full attention. This is certainly true for earth angels, who came here to earth with a specific earth angel calling.

The word *angel* alerts us to the fact that while humans who are earth angels are not actual divine angels (who exist in other dimensions like heaven and seem to only have passports to visit earth), earth angels *do* share many characteristics with heavenly angels. Heightened sensitivity, strong intuition, the ability to be easily touched or moved emotionally, and natural optimism are telltale traits of earth angels. They are also known for being non-judgmental, compassionate, supportive, and deeply concerned about the suffering of others. Both celestial and earth angels possess these qualities.

In this chapter we'll discuss further what exactly makes an earth angel an earth angel. While every earth angel you encounter will be unique and beautiful, with their own personality and their own individual destiny, earth angels often give away their secret identity by the way they carry themselves in the world.

Encountering an Earth Angel

I have told the story in my other angel books of the time I saw a divine angel—with wings and everything. Yet as I sat down to write this chapter, I was reminded of an *earth* angel I met in high school. Moving around was normal for me growing up, which looking back I feel was part of Spirit's plan. Changing towns and schools fairly often taught me resilience, showed me how to reinvent myself, and forced me to get competent at meeting and befriending strangers—all traits I have needed to fulfill my destiny.

But every time I started a new school, my sensitivity made me very aware of my vulnerable position and the energy and emotions of the other kids around me. When I was sixteen, I moved to a new state and enrolled at a new school. My last move to a new town and school had been five years previous, so I'd been settled and comfortable when I had to pick up and start again. My sensitivity was heightened at this time because part of the reason I'd moved was that my mother had been diagnosed with what was at the time a terminal illness, so she thought it would be less stressful on everyone if I went to live with my father, but I didn't want to leave the friends I'd made where I was currently living. As a sensitive person, you will find that your sensitivity may become heightened at different times in your life for different reasons. One reason your sensitivity can become heightened is because you are experiencing a significant challenge. Your heightened sensitivity may help you pick up on ways to navigate this situation. My move to another state in high school was a very difficult transition at first, but there were many moments (and people) of grace that made it successful, including an earth angel.

The first day in my new school, I clearly recall sitting in a strange classroom knowing nobody and feeling just awful. Being nervous, I'd arrived early (a common coping mechanism for sensitive people). As the rest of the kids filed into the classroom that first day, the students were mostly comfortable and confident—cracking jokes and high-fiving each other. I noticed everyone stopped to say "hello" to a girl sitting at a desk in the front of the room. She didn't seem like the prettiest girl in the class, and judging by her clothes I could tell she was not the richest—yet she was obviously the most popular.

When the teacher entered, this popular girl gathered her books, came to sit right by me, and smiled. "Hi, are you new here?" We introduced ourselves and settled in as class began. Her manner had been so open and sweet that my shoulders dropped and my heart rate calmed down. Every day afterward, this girl made a point of stopping to chat with me before class started, often choosing to sit right next to me. She would crack jokes, give me compliments, or just vent as teenagers need to. Because the others in the room saw that we were friendly, I slowly became one of the people who was high-fived before class started. One day a local restaurant near the high school handed out paper hats with their meal. The class clown had grabbed half a dozen and given them to a few others before the bell rang. As class began, I straightened my hat and looked over at my earth angel acquaintance, who was also wearing a hat. Because she had made an obvious show of befriending me, other kids in the class quickly did too. I went from no one to these kids (who had known each other their whole lives) to someone the class clown gave a paper hat to in a matter of weeks—thanks to an earth angel.

What's most interesting about this earth angel who eased my transition at that school was that she never became a close friend. I went on to have so many amazing close friends at that school—some of the most important, powerful friendships of my life started there. Yet this earth angel and I really had nothing in common (besides the fact that we were both earth angels, which we did not know back then). We liked different music, clothes, and extra-curricular activities. But we had some lovely and memorable chats in the halls and while sitting waiting for class to begin. As an earth angel, she knew the importance of getting along with all different types of people, and I believe she taught me this lesson as well.

Though this girl wasn't the prettiest or richest or funniest or smartest or most talented person at the school, she was one of the most genuine, kind, warm people there, and she was liked and respected universally. As with all earth angels, this sensitive girl who saw me sitting alone on my first day had the ability to recognize that I was intimidated and uncomfortable, despite the fact that I was trying to put on a brave front. Like all earth angels, this kind soul felt the urge to try alleviating my suffering. There was nothing in it for her—or at least nothing obvious. You see, earth angels derive deep satisfaction, purpose, and even intense joy from helping others.

My Life as an Earth Angel

Though the title of this section sounds like a juicy tabloid headline or a page-turning memoir, being an earth angel is common and not as glamorous as it sounds. The celestial angels I communicate with when I write my books or work in sessions with clients tell me that being an earth angel is a path that certain souls have chosen this lifetime, and indeed I've found it to be a deeply rewarding, phenomenally meaningful path. I think while souls evolve and grow over lifetimes, in some sense our souls are who we are; maybe earth angels are who they are, and the element of "choice" is simply about choosing to come to earth with a certain mission. Perhaps these souls have had past lives where they were not able to give back much because of life circumstances and very much long to be of service, or did things to hurt others that they regret and now they are being given the opportunity to choose a path of healing.

Part of what makes life as an earth angel so interesting is possessing an exceptional sensitivity, which translates to having exceptional intuition. This skill helps earth angels be more compassionate, because when you can sense the energy and emotions of others so immediately, you are naturally more careful with their feelings. I'd always cared about the underdog or those who were suffering, which was why I became an activist for causes I loved in high school. In my early thirties, I felt moved to help others or be of greater service and found a job at a nonprofit. Every day, I believed I was making a positive influence in the lives of people;

for the first few years of my career at that company, I honestly would have worked there for free if I didn't need to pay my bills (although I eventually experienced severe burnout there). People say to find what you would do whether you got paid for it or not, and I believed that helping others in need was mine.

My office at the nonprofit was private with a door, yet people would often come in, sit down, and tell me their troubles. "I don't know why but I always feel better after I come in here and talk to you," some coworkers told me. I think the reason people tend to seek earth angels out to talk to is because earth angels are not only very compassionate but nonjudgmental, which makes them excellent at heart-to-heart chats. Because earth angels tend to be naturally positive or optimistic, they are aces at pep talks too. The earth angel sensitivity and empathy are why people who tell their problems to an earth angel feel they are really being understood on a deep soul level.

Eventually I started helping people by giving intuitive readings one-on-one. I've found that no matter what mood I am in before I get on the phone with a client, I always experience a natural high and sense of contentment when I get off the phone at the end of a session. This feeling is a great sign that you are on purpose as an earth angel, whether you fulfill that purpose through being of service as a parent, a caretaker, a nurse, a friend, a hair stylist, a financial analyst, a dog walker, a volunteer, a teacher, or a barista.

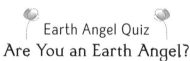

Earth Angel Quiz
Are You an Earth Angel?

Remember that if being an earth angel is not something that has so far come naturally to you, it's always an energy you can align with. Since earth angels come in all different packages from all walks of life, consider the telltale traits of earth angels represented in the quiz below to discern how aligned you currently are to earth angel energy or if you are simply a natural-born earth angel. Answer A for almost always, B for sometimes, C for hardly ever.

1. **Are you highly sensitive?** Do you pick up more easily on subtle stimuli and need a certain amount of downtime or alone time on a regular basis to reset your nervous system?

2. **Are you empathic?** Do you sometimes feel the energy and emotions of others as if this energy or emotion were your own?

3. **Do people seek out your counsel?** Are you the person at home or work or among your friends whom everyone comes to for advice or a sympathetic ear?

4. **Do you feel a close connection to Spirit?** Do angels feel real to you and is nature a place where you sense the Divine?

5. **Is helping others important to you?** Do you feel happier, more satisfied, more peaceful, or more purposeful when giving?

6. **Does the suffering of others get under your skin?** Whether it is someone in the news or in your immediate circle, does other people's pain feel important?

7. **Does life have great meaning for you?** Do you often ponder why you are here and what life is all about?

8. **Do you sometimes end up giving too much?** Is considering your boundaries with people a topic you have to revisit periodically?

9. **Are your self-care routines sacred?** Even if you don't always practice what you preach, do you notice a significant difference in your physical and emotional health when you practice healthy levels of self-care?

10. **Are you very moved by things like art, music, films, and books?** Have you been told you feel things deeply or even too deeply?

11. **Do you tend to see the cup as half full?** Are you naturally an optimist or do you find hope or gratitude in the most challenging situations or smallest experiences?

12. **Has being there for everyone else become one of your main roles?** And do you have trouble asking for help from others for yourself?

13. **Is it sometimes a challenge for you to feel calm when a loved one is hurting?** Do you have to be mindful of remaining in your own emotional skin and not letting someone else's daily experience affect yours?

Answered Mostly As—Earth Angel Whose Wings Are Showing

There is no question you are an earth angel, my friend. Welcome to the club you have probably always belonged to. You might find yourself wondering, "Do I care too much? Why am I so sensitive? What makes me different from other people I know?" Finding deep meaning in moments where others just see an ordinary experience, always looking for the hope in any situation, and caring deeply about the emotional experience of others is simply who you and all earth angels are. You aren't alone, and this book will help you navigate and enjoy life as an earth angel.

Answered Mostly Bs—Aligned with Earth Angel Energy

Congratulations—you're certainly aligned with the earth angel archetype, or it's at least playing as a background soundtrack to your life. Sometimes you might choose not to be so aligned to this energy when you are feeling drained, wanting to focus on yourself, or not wanting to be taken advantage of. Congratulations again for knowing how to protect yourself. You understand boundaries. This book will help you protect yourself even better so you can be aligned to earth angel energy all the time, and teach you to trust and value your sensitivity more so it can be a central part of your navigational system every day.

Answered Mostly Cs—Earth Angel in Training

It's not that you aren't an earth angel, just that the earth angel energy isn't very active in your life right now. You could be an earth angel in burnout mode (something covered extensively later) who gave too much or accidentally let others trample on your boundaries to the point that you've shut down your earth angel energy in an act of self-preservation. You might also be so incredibly sensitive that you fear tuning in to or helping others and just need some skills for managing and understanding your fabulous sensitivity. Hang with us for the rest of this book, and that earth angel energy will begin to resurface and shine its light outward again.

Are Earth Angels Really Divine Angels Having a Human Experience?

This seems like the ideal place to address a common misconception about divine angels. I want to start off by saying that I'm human, like you, and hardwired into this earth dimension. However, I do communicate with celestial angels every day using my intuition, and I read a lot about spirituality and philosophy. I ask the angels direct questions and receive direct answers, and I also absorb what other people are saying about angels that resonates with me. (I've written two books about celestial angels—*Angel Intuition* and *Angel Insights*.)

One of the most common questions about heavenly angels goes something like this: "My grandma died recently. Is she now an angel watching over me from heaven?" The angels have told me that they are cousins of humans, meaning they share similarities with humans but are in fact a different *species*, for lack of a better word. From what I gather, celestial angels don't become humans and humans don't become celestial angels. Humans and celestial angels are different at the soul level.

Divine angels have been known to take on human form, like in the classic film *It's a Wonderful Life*. In these situations, a celestial angel will temporarily appear as a human, like a kind pedestrian who helps someone change their tire on a deserted road or a nurse who sits by a nervous patient's bedside in a hospital. Heavenly angels only have visas to visit this dimension, so they cannot stay in human form for long, only as much time as it takes to save our buns or comfort us or point us in a new direction. Humans who pass over and then become part of your spiritual guidance squad (like your grandma who passed) and work with your divine angels are called spirit guides. These are human souls who have been on earth before.

All that said, I don't think earth angels are divine angels in training; I think earth angels volunteered for a special mission here on earth. My own divine angels are giving me a clairvoyant image of elementary school crossing guards. You might have been a crossing guard at your school or known someone who was. At some elementary schools, a few older kids might be allowed to wear reflective belts and given stop signs, and when the school bell rings to let out classes for the day, these student crossing guards help other kids (especially the youngest) cross the street in front of the school and go into the neighborhood and their homes or to their parents waiting in cars.

While all humans came here to earth to be of service, and we all have important destinies that involve touching the lives of many people, we each came here to experience and accomplish different things, as we all have unique soul missions. Part of an earth angel's collective soul mission is to help guide, support, and protect other humans. These earth angels have been deputized by the celestial angels, just like the teachers at some elementary schools deputize certain children to be crossing guards.

Earth angels share a special affinity with divine angels because they share many character traits. Possibly because of this, earth angels might be drawn to studying divine angels or connecting with them more. However, it does not follow that divine angels favor earth angels more. On a soul level, all humans are equally worthy and loveable.

An Earth Angel's Connection to the Divine

An earth angel might feel more connected to heavenly angels simply because of the earth angel's exceptional sensitivity (a topic covered in another chapter). Earth angels are hyper-perceptive and pick up more easily on subtle stimuli in their environments, an exceptional sensitivity that allows earth angels to perhaps pick up on divine guidance or the presence of a divine angel in their energy field.

Divine angels might seem more real to an earth angel, or earth angels might be more drawn to divine angels or attracted to working with them. Connecting with celestial angels or simply having a regular spiritual practice can be very nourishing and grounding for earth angels. You might have a favorite archangel you work with—archangels have incomprehensibly enormous energy signatures so they can work with infinite numbers of people at once. Therefore sensitive earth angels never need to worry that they are taking an archangel away from someone who needs their help more. Perhaps you write journal entries to your guardian angels to ask for assistance or pray to the guardian angels of your loved ones when they are in trouble. Maybe the very idea of divine angels makes you feel safe, inspired, confident, or comforted.

While I work closely with heavenly angels in my practice as an intuitive every day, I also have studied many spiritual traditions and belief systems, like the Kabbalah, Wicca, and Buddhism. If you have read this book and identify with being an earth angel, don't feel as though working with divine angels is the only path for you. There are many spiritual traditions that have so much to offer. The important thing is that you develop a spiritual practice that works for you. Your practice could include things like daily meditation and full moon rituals that don't have anything to do with divine angels, or you could incorporate divine angels into these practices. Heavenly angels would love to be a bigger part of your life in any way.

It's important to point out that divine angels do not belong to one spiritual tradition or religion. I wanted to address this early on, as I think there are cultural misconceptions that prevent people from working with divine angels or feel excluded from calling upon them. So it does not matter to a divine angel what your spiritual beliefs are, although I think we should all try to live by the golden rule, which is treating others as you would like to be treated. Living by the golden rule is very natural for earth angels, since earth angels are so often concerned with the feelings of others.

Divine angels love you with open hearts. They are happy for you to explore whatever form of spirituality feels authentic and nourishing to you. Today, many people blend spiritual ideas and traditions to find a unique personal spirituality that works for them. Or you might have grown up in a culture or religion— or just been lead to one as an adult—that resonates deeply and authentically with you, which you are committed to honoring and carrying forward for future generations.

If you are an earth angel, you might consider incorporating divine angels into your own spiritual practice, since you have so much in common. It could be as simple as inviting angels into any kind of prayer, ritual, or spiritual exercise you enjoy. You can also invite them in your thoughts and know that their presence and energy is there aiding you, protecting you, and witnessing with you.

All that divine angels ask of you is to take good care of yourself and others, a simple but not always easy to execute mandate. I know you are up to the challenge, however—when you try your best to take good care of yourself and others, you feel much more like yourself, much more alive and fulfilled and happy. Just know that your celestial angels love and stand by you no matter what— on your best and worst days. Their love is unconditional.

Earth Angels Are Good ... but They Ain't Perfect

After telling you that earth angels are more sensitive to the suffering of others, predisposed to try to comfort or uplift others, and here to help, it would be easy to imagine that earth angels are perfect, saintly, or above reproach. That is far from the truth. Earth angels are human, and even if they came here from somewhere else to be helpful, they have to be relatable. The mentors, friends, and spiritual teachers I am most attracted to and have learned the most from are not people who put themselves up on a pedestal but the folks who acknowledge openly that they are complex creatures who are wonderful and inspiring and messy and challenged all at the same time. Earth angels are not saints but are like all humans—*flawsome,* awesome in spite of and sometimes because of their flaws.

Earth angels are here just like other souls who incarnated as humans to have the full earthly experience. That experience means sometimes getting angry, behaving badly, and feeling down to the point that they cannot lift up themselves, much less anyone else. For example, earth angels can be short and rude to people because they're only human, although earth angels do feel terrible about acting this way afterward. Perhaps you've been short with a customer service representative or salesclerk because you were frustrated or running late and then spent the rest of the day (or maybe even several days) regretting it—that's typical earth angel stuff. Just try to let it go quicker.

Many people think of celestial angels as one-dimensional props, genies in a bottle who are there only to grant wishes. In my experience working with, studying, and writing about divine angels, heavenly angels are far more dynamic. Like humans, divine angels have energetic hearts and souls and personalities. Earth angels are equally dynamic. That's why it can be interesting to try to spot another earth angel—they might be in any career or at any economic status. They might be in prison, as an employee of the prison or someone incarcerated there. They might be any gender or identify as gender neutral. An earth angel might be a monk who took a vow of poverty and silence or a wild rock star with stories that would make Keith Richards blush. Earth angels could live on the other side of the world or be in the house down the street. They might have completely different ideas about politics or society or spirituality than you do. Earth angels could be someone you get along with very well, or someone you find annoying, frustrating, or challenging in some way. You might meet an earth angel in a circumstance or package that you least expect, or you might feel like you're meeting an old friend you share much in common with.

While each earth angel is a true individual, it's as important for *all* earth angels to know they are not perfect as it is for the people in their lives to know that earth angels are not perfect. Aspiring to be perfect or trying to meet an expectation that we should be better or above what is expected of a normal human is a recipe for disaster. That kind of internal attitude or projecting that kind of identity on to another is a lot of emotional pressure for an earth angel, and the emotional pressure of expectations by the earth angel's coworkers, clients, and loved ones plus the emotional pressure the earth angel puts on themselves when they sense what others expect of them is too much for anyone to handle. It's a recipe for burnout.

Earth angels are known for being nonjudgmental—or at least we can say not excessively judgmental. Earth angels tend to see the best in people and give them the benefit of the doubt. Perhaps ironically, my experience has been that earth angels can be very hard and judgmental with themselves. If you're an earth angel, cut yourself some slack. We are all doing the best we can, and if you feel like that's not true about you, then up your game. Try a little harder, but remember you came to earth to help support, love, and accept humans…and that includes supporting, loving, and accepting yourself.

If you are an earth angel who beats yourself up in your thoughts for mistakes or poor choices you made in the past, imagine that someone else had made those same mistakes or poor choices and this person came to you needing a little of your earth angel medicine. What kind, wise, encouraging, and comforting words would you offer them?

Speaking as an earth angel myself, there are many things I wish I would have handled differently in my life, times I hurt people both unknowingly and knowingly, and times I could have been kinder to others or more supportive. As I sit here to write this, a bunch of memories and images of myself behaving badly over the years are flashing before my eyes. If I could sincerely apologize to any of these people, I definitely would. As I get older, I look back on times I wish I would have behaved better or differently, but the memories that hurt the most are the times I did not support myself. As flawsome humans, we can be experts at abandoning, punishing, and sabotaging ourselves.

The divine angels I work with have told me that one of the lessons earth angels came here to learn in a big way is unconditional love. For a divine angel, unconditional love is much easier. Divine angels may not always like someone's choices, but they won't become upset with them. Divine angels can separate out the action from the individual. These angels love you and will be there for you at the drop of a feather, no matter what. They have no wish to punish anyone, and are instead here to love and support you and catch you when you fall. If you have had difficulty finding unconditional love within your family, your circle of friends, community, or romantic partners, it can be very healing to develop a closer relationship with celestial angels, as they truly do love you completely, deeply, honestly, and eternally with no strings attached.

As for earth angels, recall that they are similar to divine angels but have some significant differences. In my understanding, divine angels do not believe they are better than humans. They respect humans as powerful spiritual beings and admire us enormously, which is why they devote their existence to helping us. It takes a lot of guts for a soul to come to this dimension and live as we do. As such, an earth angel will meet people they really resent, don't agree with, and have a hard time forgiving or accepting. You, the earth angel, may not like someone else's choices or behavior *and* also not like them. I think the best way earth angels can ace that soul lesson of unconditional love is by practicing it with ourselves first. To speak of it as though it were a tree, I believe that self-love makes up an earth angel's roots. The branches represent our love of others and our ability to help others, and those branches are healthier and stronger when those self-love roots that feed and nourish the branches are healthy and strong. There is much to love about you!

Earth Angel Exercise
Increasing Self-Love

The following exercises are designed to promote more unconditional self-love in your life. While not an exact science, it's definitely an art you can get better at. The more loving you can be with yourself, the easier it will be to act lovingly toward others and spread your earth angel magic in the world.

1. **Try mirror work.** The next time you're feeling down and disappointed in yourself, go to the bathroom (being alone

works best), look in the mirror, and tell yourself out loud, "I love you." It might feel awkward the first time but do it anyway. Make eye contact with yourself, and give yourself a mischievous wink or knowing smile. If you have body issues, you can look at your body in the mirror and tell it, "I love you." Tell yourself anything else you need to hear as well, such as, "You'll do better next time," "I forgive you," or "I've got your back."

2. **Make a date with yourself.** Pick your favorite spots and activities. Go to a restaurant you love, listen to a great podcast, and spend a few hours in excellent company lingering over a delicious meal. Head to your local bookstore to browse and then have a cozy, nurturing hot drink at a café. Take yourself to a film you've been dying to see but none of your friends are interested in. Look for an art or museum exhibit you would love to get lost in for a few hours. Set out on a safe nature walk and cue up your favorite inspirational playlist as a companion. Practice great self-talk during your date, just like a supportive friend would build you up if you two were hanging out. Being able to enjoy your own company is a great sign of self-love.

3. **Pamper yourself.** A good pampering session involves something sensual (that is, gratifying to the senses). Do something to up your self-care game that you normally would not splurge on, like having a massage or pedicure. Linger in a bath of essential oils and mineral salts while listening to your favorite album. Mist your sheets with an aromatherapeutic spray before bed. Splurge on fresh flowers for the kitchen table. Do things that feel a little indulgent to increase self-love.

4. **Exchange love letters with a friend.** Earth angels tend to inspire great love in others when they put their minds to it and behave in balanced ways. Pick a close friend or family member and agree to both write a love letter to each other, describing specific character traits you love about each other with examples. You might discover something new about yourself you weren't even aware of that other people recognize and appreciate. Remind your self-love pen pal that for this particular exercise, you're not looking for tips on how to improve yourself, just lots of compliments!

Other Humans Aren't Perfect, Either

When I talk about earth angels learning to love others unconditionally, it doesn't mean having to love what they do, say, or think. Nor does it mean putting up with people treating you poorly or using you as a doormat. What I mean is recognizing the soul inside another human that is worthy and unique and important. It is from your own soul or higher self that you are able to step back from a person's actions and motivations and words and love them or wish them well from a soul level. And sometimes you have to step very far away from these folks. It's like you're saying, "On a soul level I wish you well, but I also wish you out of my life." Sometimes as a society we even have to collectively punish or try to neutralize a person because their actions, words, and so on are too toxic or harmful.

Being a human is very challenging and confusing at times, and some people act from a place of severe wounding, trauma, or mental illness. They can also be under cultural, political, familial, or religious influences that give them a distorted view of the world. Sometimes the best an earth angel can do is simply acknowledge that another person has a soul, pray for them to be healed or see the light, and then move away. And sometimes earth angels will not be capable of even this. They might have some intense anger, grief, or confusion they need to process. Above all, being an earth angel in relationships with others does not mean you have to tolerate toxic behavior or being treated with disrespect. Your emotional and physical safety and well-being should always be your top priority and concern.

Earth Angels Get No Free Passes

By this point, some of you might be thinking that you are in fact an earth angel. Or you felt that you were definitely an earth angel the moment you picked up this book. Maybe you were already familiar with the concept long before this book came out. Still others might be realizing that their spouse, child, best friend, aunt, grandparent, or high school guidance counselor is/was an earth angel. Any earth angels out there or people who know one well can attest to the fact that life for an earth angel is not easy or free from suffering.

It's my belief that all of our souls came to earth with specific lessons, experiences, roles, and relationships planned out for us. I also believe that some things are decided on the fly, or spontaneously by our guides and our own free will. There is wiggle room and even room to renegotiate some soul contracts or agreements your soul made with yourself and Spirit before you incarnated on earth. Think of your life as having many opportunities to cocreate with Spirit or help steer the ship in a direction you would like to head.

Also on this earth is a lot of suffering. Since all humans here are wired into this dimension for this lifetime, no one goes untouched by suffering, nor is it something you can navigate around. If one of every earth angel's soul contracts is to help love, support, and encourage other humans, then surely earth angels will be called to places where people are suffering, whether it means helping an individual grieving over a loved one's passing or a whole society dealing with widespread natural disasters and famine.

Are earth angels doomed to experience more suffering than others simply because they are earth angels? Certainly not. But I do believe earth angels were meant to roll up their sleeves and get down in the muck of life to help others who are struggling. This could look like helping to raise a family of children, guiding them through all the peaks and valleys growing up entails, or it could look like being a political activist who devotes their whole life to a cause they're passionate about, or it could look like being the person in an office who helps keep people cheered up and motivated and peaceful every day. Each earth angel will feel or be called to serve in a unique way.

Earth angels might develop their deep compassion and empathy by having personal life experiences that are traumatic or challenging. This could include dysfunctional childhoods, illnesses, or major setbacks in life that cause earth angels to have more empathy for the suffering of others. These experiences are not part of an earth angel's journey to punish or test them but rather to help inform and educate them. The best way you can help people who are suffering is truly understanding their pain. I'm *not* saying that earth angels were singled out to feel more pain or experience more challenges than others; these things—pain and challenge— are a natural part of earthly life. For an earth angel, these experiences can help deepen their empathy, aiding them in one of their most important life missions.

Some people out there might have experienced very traumatic things in childhood, or faced devastating, long illnesses. Having experienced my share of these things, I get it if you feel angry and hurt about your experiences. Just because you've had them does not mean you are an earth angel, as I think we all deal with our share of suffering. Above all, I would never try to justify someone's suffering by saying it was an important lesson, a karmic repercussion, or part of Spirit's plan. Nothing about destiny or suffering is so simple or easily explained. I personally hate to see suffering, just like heavenly angels hate suffering. Sometimes divine angels can help ease our suffering in dramatic ways, and sometimes their wings are tied. Sometimes the best celestial angels can do is simply stand by us in our suffering and send us grace opportunities to heal and move on.

Perhaps simply by helping people who are suffering, you as an earth angel will experience some form of secondary suffering. If you're reading this book right now and are suffering, please connect with your divine angels. No matter what challenges you will face, Spirit is available to you. Know that divine angels can always exert some form of influence over your situation, and ask to see proof of it.

As an earth angel, you were intended to have the full human experience, which includes moments of deep satisfaction, comfort, joy, love, humor, freedom, and excitement. As earth angels are sensitive and tend to feel things in an immediate way, these peak experiences and moments of happiness will be very special. Earth angels were never meant to be martyrs, so if you identify as an earth angel I encourage you to take every chance at happiness you can find. Ask your heavenly angels to help position you for more positive experiences, and treat yourself well any and every way you can. Make space for the things you love to do, make time to spend with the people you love, and work on loving yourself more. Remember that the help, support, comfort, and love of your divine angels is simply one thought, prayer, meditation, or journal entry away.

Earth Angel Exercise
Asking for Assistance from Your Divine Angels

Earth angels should know that getting help from heaven is just a connection away. You can connect with a simple thought during your morning commute to work, like, "I need help staying calm and confident in this meeting today." You could also say a formal prayer where you light a candle and pray, sit at your home altar and pray, say a silent prayer before your daily meditation, or close your eyes and bow your head while you pray.

Journaling is a powerful way to connect with your celestial angels and activate more divine guidance and intervention in your life. It's also a wonderful way to check in with yourself about what you need and want. This is especially important for earth angels, as they tend to think about others before considering themselves. Try this divine angel-activating journal exercise the next time you are going through a challenge and need angelic support, when you want help achieving a dream, when you are ready to surrender the outcome of a situation to heaven, or once a week as a way to connect with heavenly angels and become a more powerful cocreator in your life.

Step 1. Create a sacred atmosphere.
Don't overthink this step. It's really about creating a calm, quiet environment where you can better connect and focus. This exercise is best done on your own when there isn't a lot of noise and

bustle around. How do you create a sacred atmosphere? Perhaps you like to put on soothing music, burn incense, hold a crystal, have reminders of nature like fresh flowers around, journal on the day of the full or new moon, or gaze at an angel figurine. Use this step as an invitation to be more mindful about what makes you feel connected to your soul and Spirit.

Step 2. Tell your divine angels what you're grateful for.

Grab your journal and something to write with. Even if life has been incredibly challenging, or you are desperately yearning for a shift or positive change, take a few sentences or a whole paragraph and write down what you are grateful for right now. It might be something you normally take for granted, like shelter and food, or it might be something out of the ordinary that happened recently, like a financial windfall or a new friend coming into your life. This step raises your vibration, which is better for manifesting; an energy of gratitude has a more positive and most of all more *open* energy signature. Gratitude will also improve your mood. Keep in mind that you can be grateful at the same time you are allowing yourself to process difficult emotions like anger or sadness.

Step 3. Ask for help from your divine angels.

Earth angels love to help others, but it's important for *you* to get in the habit of asking for help too. Pour your heart out here about how you would like heavenly angels to help and why. It's fine to get specific with the kind of help you require, e.g., "I'd like four new clients this month that I can really be of service to" or "I want a 4 percent raise at work because I'd really like to start saving for a house." At the same time, stay open and flexible. Sometimes the angels will answer your prayer in a way you never expected. This is partly true because angels have to work with whatever ingredients are in your life and available at the moment. For example, maybe your company has just decided to put a freeze on raises. As well, it's possible that something that's even better for you than what you requested is also out there. There could be another job that you would also enjoy that pays more, or some side hustle that could bring you more money than a raise *and* more purpose and fulfillment.

Step 4. Look for guidance from your divine angels regarding this issue.

Thank your celestial angels in your journal and then watch for synchronicities or meaningful coincidences showing up around this issue, new opportunities showing up around this issue, or intuitive hits from your own sixth sense about how to proceed regarding this issue that were sent from heavenly angels. Think like a mystical detective and examine your life for clues from your divine angels. Intuitive hits can come as a calm, gentle voice in your mind; a breakthrough or a-ha! idea; an image that appears in your mind; a gut instinct or strong feeling; or an intuitive dream while you sleep. Pay close attention to things loved ones, colleagues, or even strangers say to you regarding this issue. Angels love to speak to us through the people in our lives. Watch for anything new showing up.

Awakening the Earth Angel Inside

When did you first realize you were an earth angel? Was it when you read the back of this book, or when you were a small child? Many sensitive people feel they are somewhat "different" than other children but don't have the language to express how exactly. I had a client once years ago who I thought was an earth angel.

Normally when I tell someone they are an earth angel, I have to quickly follow that observation up with an explanation of what an earth angel is. Yet this client responded to my observation that she was an earth angel with an immediate and emphatic, "Oh, yes!" So maybe you have been reading along already quite familiar with this energy and how it operates in your life.

Earth angel energy might be something we sense or see evidence of looking back at our own childhood, but many times it's something you grow into, just as you grow into yourself. I had a client recently in his eighties who was marveling at the fact that he was still learning important life lessons at this stage of his journey. You might step into your earth angel energy when you are sixteen or when you are sixty. Perhaps it's a slow blossoming all along the way, or you might experience quick growth spurts. We are constantly changing, growing, and evolving, and it is what keeps life interesting.

A certain event—for example, a major disappointment, losing a loved one, being given an important opportunity in your career, or attending an inspiring workshop—could have awakened your earth angel energy. Your earth angel energy might have been awakened at a certain age, like when your Saturn returns astrologically in your late twenties and early thirties, a time when many people step more into their calling or start taking their life seriously (or *even more* seriously.)

If you know someone who you think has earth angel energy—a compassionate and giving nature mixed with heightened sensitivity and empathy—you might give them an invitation to the club they are, unknowingly, already a member of.

Activating and Aligning to Earth Angel Energy

Whether everything I have written so far resonated deeply with you and you think being an earth angel is central to your destiny, or you simply believe that getting more in touch with earth angel energy can be rewarding or help you on your life path, these tips will prove valuable guideposts. Sometimes the most natural-born earth angel can begin to feel lost in the world and even worse feel lost inside themselves. Doing the following can make you feel more grounded, centered in your own energy, happy, and purposeful.

- **Do something nice for someone else where the only reward will be knowing you made someone's day better or easier.** Send a card to a friend, smile at your cashier, leave a bigger than normal tip, offer to take something off a coworker's plate, tell someone in your life what you admire about them.

- **Be merciful.** Give someone a second chance or the benefit of the doubt. Put yourself in their shoes, which is something easy for earth angels to do since they are so sensitive and empathic. Ask yourself how you would want to be treated if you were in this situation—and be merciful with yourself.

- **Connect with your celestial angels.** Earth angels feel more peaceful, safe, and confident when they remember their special connection to divine angels. Listen to music about angels (there is a great playlist in the back of this book) or watch a movie or read a book about divine angels. Give your guardian angels (we all have more than one) nicknames or pick one archangel to work with. Popular archangels who come into my sessions to assist clients include Michael, who can help you feel more protected and courageous; Raphael, who can promote healing in any area of your life—relationships, finances, etc.; and Chamuel, who can encourage peacefulness.

• **Look for more meaning in your life.** As an earth angel, finding purpose and meaning in your days is essential. View your life symbolically and watch for themes that have been showing up lately. You'll always be given nudges to change and grow. Is Spirit sending you messages to take better care of yourself, be careful about the words you use with others, dream bigger, slow down, reconcile with an estranged loved one, start a creative project, move homes, reexamine your career, give back, or take a chance on love?

• **Be aware of your effect on others.** Earth angels are like all humans in the sense that they will have bad days and good days; sometimes you'll be very proud of the way you behaved and other times, not so much. Yet earth angels are exceptionally attuned to how they can positively affect others. Remember that sometimes your words or even your presence can be a significantly positive part of someone else's day.

• **Honor your sensitivity and heightened sixth sense.** Earth angels are highly sensitive and empathic (discussed more in the next chapter), so they pick up on intuitive information others may have missed. Don't discount this information, like when you get a gut instinct about a person or situation. Nourish and respect this sensitivity by taking good care of your physical body. Take good care of your nervous system: avoid unnecessary drama and get plenty of rest and retreat time.

• **Acknowledge your heart.** Earth angels have a lot of heart energy, which means you might feel things deeply, such as great excitement for a friend who is getting married or great disappointment if you don't get that job offer. You might be the kind of person who cries easily or actively worries about suffering in the world. Always listen to your heart and the information it sends, but balance it by consulting the information coming from your head, too, especially when making big decisions.

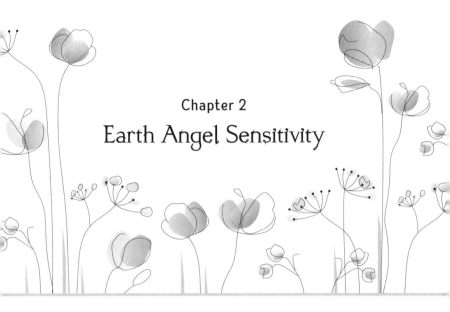

Chapter 2
Earth Angel Sensitivity

In this chapter, we'll explore sensitivity in depth, the earth angel's radar. Being sensitive is a gift but one that *really* should come with an instruction manual. Unfortunately, most of us unwrap the gift of sensitivity in childhood without any explanation of who we are or how to operate within our families or in the larger world.

The usual way is to figure out how to navigate through trial and error. If we're lucky, another sensitive person in the family who is older and wiser and can help guide us, or our parents read up about sensitive children as a way to understand us better. Often by adulthood, those who were sensitive even as children have begun to put the pieces of their puzzle together and begin to feel comfortable and even confident in their sensitivity.

You might have come into your sensitivity not in childhood but much later in life. Sensitivity evolves and changes throughout our lives, and I have witnessed many clients experiencing sensitivity growth spurts. This is like a physical growth spurt in that it's very awkward and disorienting at first. Over time, however, you'll become comfortable with this new level of increased sensitivity.

Please consider this chapter and chapter 3 to be an owner's manual to sensitivity. As well, there's a lot of information out there. So many exceptional books have been written about sensitivity. The recommended reading section has a list of other resources for sensitive souls. If you are interested in more information specifically on intuition or your sixth sense, consider exploring my book on the topic, *Angel Intuition*. We are fortunate enough to be living in a time when sensitivity is being more widely discussed and understood.

What Is Sensitivity?

Sensitivity is a word that has many different meanings to many different people. You might have first encountered this word in childhood, when someone told you, "Oh, stop being so sensitive." The implication was that you were taking things too personally. I have noticed among my clients that sensitive people tend to take things personally *but* not in the same way that people with narcissistic tendencies take things personally. Sensitive people might just get their feelings hurt a bit more easily. Because sensitive people are easily attuned to the energy and emotions of others, they might take comments or actions not directed at them more personally.

If you cry easily at movies or headlines in the news, you may have been called sensitive. If you have difficulties processing certain foods or drinks, you may have been called sensitive. If you like your office at a certain temperature or things at home in a certain order, you could have been called sensitive. If you are easily overwhelmed by anyone around you experiencing strong emotions or energy, you may have been called sensitive.

You might have heard various terms to describe people who are sensitive. These might include *highly sensitive person* (HSP), *empath*, and *earth angel*. Here we'll clarify each. Bear in mind that these terms can have a certain fluidity or overlap; as sensitivity becomes more accepted and studied, we are learning more about these evolving concepts. As we'll be exploring sensitivity in depth over the next two chapters, I won't differentiate between HSPs, empaths, and earth angels, after this; instead I'll simply use the term *sensitive*.

Highly sensitive people are hyper-perceptive, meaning they pick up more easily on subtle stimuli in their environments. Dr. Elaine Aron published what remains the definitive book on the subject, *The Highly Sensitive Person*, in the mid-1990s. We might explain how HSPs function by saying their nervous systems gather more information. This information could be physical information like smells and sounds, or it could be even more subtle information like the energy of a room or another person's feelings. For HSPs, stimulation can register more strongly and powerfully, so the annoying car alarm going off in the background is even more irritating or the coworker who cannot refrain from chattering away is even more distracting. HSPs therefore prefer environments of low stimulation, like a quiet office where they can focus on the details of their work, or an orderly home where the clutter of daily life does not feel overwhelmingly distracting. It seems that highly sensitive people are simply naturally wired this way. However, some people might be naturally wired to be highly sensitive but have learned to numb or ignore their senses to cope and won't act much like HSPs. If this describes you, play with environments of higher and lower stimulation to see what you might naturally prefer.

Some (but certainly not all) highly sensitive people might also be **empaths**. Likewise, people who are empaths may or may not identify as highly sensitive. Empaths feel other people's emotions and energy and sometimes even other people's physical states as if they were their own. This is a term that has become more popular in recent years; Dr. Judith Orloff wrote an important book on the subject called *The Empath's Survival Guide* (2017). As an example of an empath's experience, if I am in a session with a client who has issues with their knees, I may feel a brief ache in my knees when I get on the phone with them. If they have issues in their stomach, I may feel a funny sensation in my own stomach as I talk to them. Fortunately, this only happens for a few moments either right before I get on the phone with a client or during our call. It only lasts long enough for my intuition to give me information about what is going on with my client. "Has something been going on with your shoulder?" I once asked a client, suddenly feeling the need to stretch and rotate my left shoulder. "Yes," he replied. "It has been stiff and sore."

It's more common for empaths to simply be very good at tuning in to the energy and emotions of others. This is something I do before I get on the phone with a client. From a first-time client whom I know nothing about, I can sense before I get on the phone that this person has a playful energy, for example, or perhaps a very serious energy. I might also sense that they are excited or sad or anxious, and the reason why (e.g., excited or sad or anxious about a romantic issue). Empaths can also pick up more easily on the energy of a situation or a room. Because empaths are so excellent at emotionally and energetically putting themselves into someone else's metaphorical shoes, they have to watch out not to merge psychologically with other people. An empath's default wiring is to tune in to others, so it is important for all empaths to learn techniques to help them mindfully tune in and out to certain degrees. For more about empaths, see my book *Self-Care for Empaths.*

Earth angels are both highly sensitive and empathic. Their ability to sense so much also makes them incredibly compassionate and want to help others. All HSPs and empaths are special, wonderful people. Each of us has an important role here on earth tailored to us specifically, and we were each meant to be of service. Earth angels seem to feel a deep need to be incredibly giving, and their sensitivity helps them identify who needs their help and what exactly is required. Being an HSP, an empath, or both does not mean that you are an earth angel. There might be another important role you were meant to play here on earth, or you may not yet have tapped into your earth angel energy. Personally, it wasn't until I was in my early thirties that I became aware of and then devoted myself to the earth angel path.

Sensitivity and Intuition

Sometimes people tell me, "I think I might be intuitive enough to do what you do: get on the phone with people and receive guidance about what is going on with them and what might help. But I couldn't handle tuning in to so many people that way." These folks are very empathic or clairsentient (feeling any intuitive information) and fear that tuning in to too many people will overwhelm them.

In sessions with clients, I am not only using the clairsentient psychic pathway but also clairaudience (hearing guidance), clair-cognizance (knowing guidance), and clairvoyance (seeing guid-ance). Sensitive earth angels are very strong in the clairsentient psychic pathway, but you might also be strong in any of the other three. As you study and work with your intuition, also called your sixth sense, any of the other three psychic pathways might open up for you.

The four main psychic pathways are:

- **Clairaudience:** This is when you hear a voice in your mind that is not your own. The voice will never sound threatening or talk constantly in an annoying or disruptive way asso-ciated with people who are suffering from mental illness, hormone imbalance, severe vitamin and mineral deficien-cies, or other medical issues. This voice will sound calm and the same no matter who is giving you this intuitive infor-mation—it could be coming from anyone on your spiri-tual guidance squad (your divine angels, loved ones who've passed on, Spirit, your own higher self, or ascended masters like Mary or Buddha). Clairaudience and clairvoyance are the rarer psychic pathways to naturally present themselves.

- **Clairvoyance:** Have you ever seen an image in your mind that gave you important information about a situation or answered a question? This is called clairvoyance, and the pictures you see could be straightforward or a metaphor that requires a bit of interpretation. Dreams can also be a great source of intuitive guidance, however clairvoyant images appear in your mind when you are awake. Although this is, like clairaudience, one of the two rarer psychic pathways to naturally present itself, you can try opening up the clairvoyant psychic pathway by doing guided meditations or asking your celestial angels to send you clairvoyant images during your usual meditation practice.

• **Claircognizance:** The intellectual psychic pathway, clair-cognizance will bring intuitive thoughts and a-ha! ideas into your mind. Pay close attention to the thoughts that appear out of the blue or are fully formed, as well as the thoughts that seem like out-of-the-box breakthroughs. These thoughts were probably not deduced or generated by your logical mind but are important intuitive insights. Try not to second-guess these thoughts or let your logical mind dismiss them. Instead, sit with the possibility of them being genuine solutions or explanations arrived at intuitively.

• **Clairsentience:** I love this psychic pathway because it is the most common to naturally present itself and one that earth angels are very strong in. Earth angels will automatically be attracted to working with this psychic pathway because it's all about feeling or sensing intuitive guidance. Being able to sense the energy and emotions of other people falls into this category, as does the ability to sense whether an opportunity, situation, or decision is right for you. If you get the feeling that now isn't the best time to ask your boss for a raise or that a friend is really down and needs more TLC, this is information coming from the clairsentient branch of your intuitive system.

Learning how to more mindfully tune in and out of others, a matter explored throughout this book, is one way clairsentient people can avoid becoming overwhelmed by the energy and emotions of others, whether those other people are the sensitive earth angels' clients or simply people standing next to them in the grocery line.

I once had a friend who hated to go to spiritual services, not because she wasn't spiritual, but because the places she went encouraged people to hold hands before the services (which is common). If a bunch of people were in a circle holding hands, she would start to feel an energy overload, as if her very empathic circuits were picking up on the energy and emotions of everyone in that circle. These empaths might also be more sensitive to collective world energy and the way energetic cycles move through the world.

Surely sensitivity exists on a spectrum, just as intuitive ability can exist on a spectrum. Your level of sensitivity and intuitive ability can also change throughout your life. You might go through a period where you have been so stressed or busy, eating and drinking so poorly, or so wrapped up in an addictive behavior like binge shopping that you end up a little numbed out to your sensitivity. Likewise, I've had clients seek me out because their sensitivity and intuition had suddenly increased and they were having trouble managing them. An increase in sensitivity due to a life event, spiritual awakening, increased self-care, or study of intuition and sensitivity can be mildly disorienting at first, but it always comes into balance and you'll get up to speed so that the new level of sensitivity feels normal and is not distracting. If your new level of sensitivity doesn't naturally come into balance, don't be afraid to talk to someone knowledgeable to get assistance.

Sensitive and Misunderstood

When we talk about sensitivity, we are not talking about how certain people experience or process emotions but how they experience and process *everything*, as well as how their nervous systems are wired. Sensitive people might have been told growing up that they were "thin-skinned," which is actually a great way to describe sensitive people and how they experience the world. Where some people have a thicker outer layer that blocks more of other people's emotions and energy and stimuli in the environment, sensitive people have a more permeable membrane that allows more data to come in. I don't think anyone likes to be micromanaged at work, but sensitive people might have an especially tough time in this scenario as a manager's anxious or overbearing energy registers even stronger with the sensitive employee.

Because sensitive people simply perceive more and pick up more easily on subtle stimuli, a sensitive child might pick up more quickly on subtle cues that there is a problem in their parents' marriage. In the case of earth angels, these people were obviously wired to pick up on more for a reason. The more you can perceive of someone else's experience, the more you can empathize with them and the more you want to help them.

In the past, when someone was described as *sensitive*, there was a connotation that this person was weak or fragile. In fact, I got very angry and defensive the first time a close friend in college insisted that I was sensitive! As someone who has a strong warrior archetype soul and is quite assertive and independent, my first thought was that my friend was implying that I couldn't handle certain things. This misconception about being weak or fragile might have come about because sensitive people have finely tuned nervous and energetic systems that pick up on a lot. After a big event like a wedding, or even a busy day at the office interacting with many people, the sensitive soul will require some low-stimulation downtime. The sensitive person simply perceived and picked up on more during the day than someone who is not as sensitive, so their system is more overstimulated and needs adequate time to cool down, much like an overheated engine.

Sensitive people are so affected by their environment that after leaving a busy office or wedding venue, for example, the quickest way to calm themselves is to go into a calming environment—a room where they can be alone, read a book, or listen to soft music. Sensitive people can absorb the energy around them very easily, something that can be used to their benefit. If you are feeling down, go to a café for lunch where people are laughing and chatty or curl up on the couch and watch a funny movie. If you are feeling stressed, go to a yoga studio where the vibes are peaceful and grounded or take a long walk in nature.

Being sensitive is not as complex as it might seem. Simply think of yourself as having a broader bandwidth than other people. As we continue to explore sensitivity, you will find coping skills and navigational tools that will help you manage and make the most of this special character trait.

Sensitive people:

- Are very attuned to the energy and emotions of others.
- Like to have an adequate amount of alone or retreat time.
- Negotiate the balance between being out in the world and healthy retreat time.
- May be easily moved by things in their own lives or even things they see in films, read about in books, or take in from the news.
- Might have always felt they were different even since childhood.

- Can go through periods of heightened sensitivity as well as periods where they feel more numb.

- Might have discovered or activated their sensitivity through a life event or spiritual awakening.

- Come in all kinds of packages and practice all kinds of different professions.

- Are more easily affected by their physical environments and the people around them.

- Pick up on lots of subtle intuitive information others might miss.

- Might register elements of their physical environment in a stronger way, like sounds, tastes, smells, temperatures, et cetera.

- Are *not* weak or fragile.

Being Sensitive Is Nothing to Be Scared About or Run From

You will occasionally hear people describe themselves as empaths this way: "Oh, I can't handle (a stressful situation). I'm an empath." While it's true that people who identify as highly sensitive or empathic may prefer certain types of work or home environments, I guarantee that there are sensitive people all over the world at this very moment teaching roomfuls of rambunctious children, waiting tables in busy cafes, counseling people in emergency room psych wards, competing in high stakes athletic sports, working long hours on Wall Street, and mediating between divorcing couples. It takes all kinds of people in all kinds of roles to make the world go round. Definitely find what fits and works for *you*. And if you are highly sensitive or empathic or both, please know that it does not have to stop you from doing whatever you believe is your calling or destiny in this life.

Ideally, a sensitive person will know their own personal sweet spots—how much stimulation they can personally handle, and the overstimulation cues from their own system. Let me tell you something: it's no fun to be a sensitive person who is incredibly overwhelmed, but it's also no fun to be a sensitive person who is *underwhelmed*. You want your life to be interesting and engaging and contain a certain level of excitement, no matter what type of person you are.

Sometimes sensitive people can have a tendency to isolate and spend too much time alone or in low-stimulation settings. They are trying to find the right balance, and everyone's will be different. You'll know you've found the right balance of stimulation when you don't feel too bored or too stressed. This balance might look like planning out your weeks or months professionally and socially to make sure there is adequate space between deadlines and events, *and* also enough going on that you feel connected and engaged.

The balance is never perfect. You will have days that are *really* overstimulating—the kids are going nuts, your boss is on the warpath, you forgot to pay a bill on time and your spouse is freaking out over the late fee. Follow up a day like that with some recovery time. You might work in an office where there is a big deadline at the end of every month, like the publication of a monthly magazine. The days leading up to the monthly deadline could be a slow build of writing stories, gathering photos and artwork, and designing pages, so the last week of the month is fairly hectic. A sensitive employee would want to take the first week of the month—after the last month's magazine is out the door and when the next month's magazine is still in the planning stages—as slow and easy as possible. That could allow their system recovery time after that hectic deadline. By the end of the first week of the month, the sensitive employee might feel calm and rested and ready to do it all over again.

A stressful or overstimulating situation might go on for a while—you might be in cancer treatment or having to stick it out at a job you really hate or going through a lengthy divorce. Find regular calm spots of low stimulation to sustain you through this time. As a sensitive person, you will need some retreat and recovery time—even a small amount counts—built in every day. *Retreat and recovery* is a phrase I will be using throughout the book to describe how sensitive people retreat into a low-stimulation environment so that their sensitive systems can recover from being overstimulated. If you're in the middle of a prolonged challenge, think of yourself as a marathon runner and the peaceful times you carve out for yourself as the drinks of water and orange slices that will get you through this race.

Sensitive people were never meant to hide away and avoid all stressful situations. This is especially true of earth angels, who came here to roll up their sleeves and help other humans through the grittiness of earthly life. We all know how it feels when we are in our sweet spot, when life chugs along and we feel positive and calm. If you're not in your sweet spot, don't be afraid to reach out to others or experiment and do whatever you need to get to that sweet spot. Just remember that as an earth angel, you are a sensitive person who came here to engage with the world.

Earth Angels Honor the Power of Energy

Sensitive people know that humans don't just have a physical body, but an energetic body too. For earth angels, someone's vibes are not just a woo-woo concept but an energy the earth angel can pick up, feel, and read. Have you ever passed someone in your neighborhood, at a party, in the hallway at school, or in a conference room at work whom you had a crush on and felt the energy around you suddenly become heightened and electric? Odds are this other person felt the energy shift too. Your mutual attraction created a special energy when your two energy bodies passed each other.

Earth angels are particularly adept at picking up on energy, which you can use to your advantage. If you are picking up on energy that your child is lying to you about something important, this is good information to have. If you pick up on energy that the salesperson you are working with truly cares that you are satisfied with the product they are selling, this is also useful information. Earth angels should trust their hunches about energy. While we can always be wrong about the energy we pick up—someone's avoidance of us or nervousness around us might mean they actually like us quite a bit—the energy you pick up from people, places, and situations is part of how an earth angel navigates the world.

Be Mindful of Energy's Cocreative Potential

Think about the energy you want to bring to a situation ahead of time. If you must have a difficult talk with your coworker or spouse, it might be worth coming to the conversation with an open and friendly energy. People tend to mirror the energy that we meet them with. This is an unconscious reflex for most people, especially people who do not think too much about energy or its affects.

If you know your boss is angry with you, meet them with an energy of respect and openness instead of defensiveness and intensity. As you keep sitting in that calm, diplomatic energy, it can have a dramatic effect on the energy your boss sends you. Practice being more mindful of the energy you send a situation and see what results.

Choosing your energy won't always be possible. Sometimes your emotions will be too intense, and that's okay. Emotions are important to honor, even—and maybe especially—the challenging ones. I've found that people who study energy and practice creating it have intensely powerful energy signatures. They are therefore more easily able to affect the energy of a space or group of people in positive ways. So the more you learn about and work with energy, the stronger and more influential your own energy will become.

Earth Angel Exercise
Influencing the Energy of a Situation

You can do this energy exercise without even being near the person whose energy you want to affect or the location where you want to change the energy around.

Step 1. Picture the situation you want to influence the energy around being positive.

If you're a teacher, picture the students in the class you are teaching, for example, feeling excited to be there and paying close attention to what you say. Imagine them raising their hands to ask questions to show they are engaged. If you're a student presenting a paper, imagine the other students in the audience listening with interest and respect. See if you are able to positively affect the energy of your classroom and the people in it by meditating on the images and energy you would like to see in this classroom. Part of what you are doing here is creating a change in your own perception of the classroom, which will naturally change your energy when you are next physically there. This positive change in your energy will help positively influence the energy of others in the classroom.

Step 2. Do your part to help create the energy you want to experience.

In the classroom examples above, if you were the teacher you might smile and say an enthusiastic hello to kids as they enter your class, or get to know their personalities so you can bond with them more easily. If you were the student presenting a paper, you would make your presentation interesting and relevant and probably practice in front of people to see if there are any ways you could up your public speaking game, like with humor or getting the audience to participate.

Step 3. Do something that is an energetic match for the energy you want to create.

If you're wanting a classroom to be drama-free, do something the night before class that makes you feel warm and peaceful, like curling up to watch your favorite movie, lighting some candles and listening to a great album, laughing on the phone with a friend, or walking your dog along a safe beach. As you wake up the next day, you will still have some of that calm energy you created the night before in your system, which will help set the tone for your day in class.

It's All About the Vibes

Earth angels might be attracted to certain lovers, friends, or physical spaces because of the vibes they give off. Your favorite coffee spot might be all about how nice and warm the collective energy of the baristas is (and their tips might reflect that energy as well). You might like a certain business partner because their energy is so intense. This go-getter vibe made you want to sign on to their project right away. You might have been attracted to friends because of their fun-loving and relaxed energy, or because they have a compassionate and nonjudgmental energy.

Keep in mind that life and energy are organic, so vibes can change. You have no doubt experienced this in the workplace—an office or company that once was a delight to work at becomes toxic. This can happen when management switches styles, the workload increases, money becomes tight, or the employees start to feel the workplace is stagnant. The change in vibes at your workplace might also be due to more personal reasons. I knew someone once who loved the company she was hired by, stayed there for a decade, and worked her way up the ladder to a management position. Then one day, it just didn't feel right anymore. After months turned into a year of it not feeling right anymore, she made some big changes in her life. For her, it meant going down to working less than forty hours a week at the company and changing her role as manager so she could go back to school.

The vibes of relationships can change too, and a close friend you always looked forward to hanging out with in the past can become someone whose texts you now avoid. Though it can be hard when good vibes turn bad, it's important to admit it.

Check in with the vibes of a situation periodically, just like a doctor will take your temperature whenever you stop by for a wellness visit. A family member who has been prickly to you in the past may now be in a different space or have a different opinion of you, and the vibes between you are more pleasant.

Use Your Feelers to Discern the Vibes or Energy

Isn't it funny how people don't even have to say anything for you to get a sense of their energy? I have found that before I even get on the phone with a new client, I get an idea of their energy, their personality, and what kind of vibe they are giving off. It's like my feelers are stretching out through time and space to tune in to their energy. In fact, *feelers* is a term I will use to describe how sensitive people pick up on other folks' energy and emotions empathically. While your feelers will always be active, sensitive people can choose when to put their feelers out further or extend them, like a bug does, to use their sensitivity to give them extra data. This is something I do in a session with a client. You might choose to put your feelers out when talking to a client of your own, or when meeting up for lunch with a new friend to get a better sense of where they are coming from emotionally and energetically.

You might be drawn to someone because your feelers pick up that their energy is off or low or negative. You may sense that someone is sad and needs a lift, or that a mask of anger is really hiding the fact that someone is scared and needs support. Since earth angels love to help people who are struggling, it may be that someone's challenging energy is what draws you to them.

Whatever energy you are picking up with your feelers, remember that being able to sense and read energy is part of your sensitivity. This is not useless information, and it is not information that is meant to shut down your sensitivity—although it might overwhelm you. If you find the energy of a room or person over-whelming, try tuning in to something different. Shift your focus, like tuning in to the coworker who is upbeat and calm over the one who is stressed and harried. A common way we tune in to a person or situation is simply by thinking about them. So in the example of a coworker who is stressed and harried, not only limit your inter-actions with this person but limit the amount of time you think about them. Leave thoughts of work at work, and don't take them home with you or into your lunchbreak, for example.

As a sensitive you do not have to be at the mercy of someone else's energy, or even your own funky energy. Yet being able to pick up easily on energy and vibes is simply part of being an earth angel. Accept that as a fact of life for you and learn how to work with it, which we will cover in the following exercise.

Earth Angel Exercise
Shifting Your Energy and Lifting Your Vibration
Raising your vibration can help you feel more peaceful, protected, and powerful in the world. Here are some steps to take if you are in an energy funk, either from your own energy or someone else's:

Step 1: Discern if there are any challenging emotions you have been avoiding processing.
Have you been swallowing your disappointment over not getting a job you interviewed for or having a friend you're crushing on tell you they think you two are better off as "just friends"? If you are feeling angry, sad, or in any way emotionally triggered, give yourself some space to feel into and process these challenging emotions. Once this is done you might feel much lighter energet-ically as well as more calm or hopeful. Remember that sometimes

really wonderful events, like someone you love asking you to marry them or getting your dream job, can also cause challenging emotions like anxiety.

Step 2: Do an energy clearing of yourself or your space.

Put on some gentle sacred music and ask your heavenly angels to fill you with lovely, soft, peaceful energy. Take a shower and lather yourself with soap that has an invigorating or calming scent. Get out in nature and tune in to the energy of the trees, sky, and water around you simply by paying close attention to its details: the color of the leaves, the feel of wind on your face, the smell of salty ocean. Clear the energy of your home or office by giving it a clean or tidying up, burning some sage or incense, placing a crystal or fresh flowers in the room, or all of these.

Step 3: Absorb something inspiring.

A wonderful thing about earth angels is they have the ability to really take things in and take them to heart. Listen to a podcast or watch a video from one of your favorite inspirational authors. Give yourself an oracle card reading with your most uplifting deck. Read a book about potential and possibility or manifesting that excites you. In these ways you can connect with something or someone that has the kind of vibration or energy you want to be feeling.

Step 4. Examine your self-care.

Is there something in your self-care routine that's been off lately? This can make your energy feel off too. Have you been eating and sleeping well? Are you taking the medications and supplements you know work for you? Maybe you have been skipping some important self-care rituals, like quiet time alone, a monthly massage, a weekly yoga class, a creative hobby, staying on top of your bills, or connecting with friends. Up your self-care game if your energy has felt funky.

Step 5: Ask your intuition if anyone or anything has been draining your energy.

This step is crucial: Get quiet and tune in to who or what might have been draining you. Maybe you see an image of a family member's face and realize worrying about their addiction struggles has been draining you. Perhaps you hear your partner's name in your mind and realize that their rants about not being able to move up at work have been majorly draining you. A gut instinct might tell you that your child's wild afternoon playdates have been frazzling your nerves, or you might have a thought that your morning commute or worrying about money has been more draining than you realized. Once you identify what has been draining your energy most, you can take steps to approach these people and situations differently. You might have to change the nature of your child's playdates, for example, to an activity like reading that is more calming. Or you might watch your thoughts and only allow yourself to ponder your worries long enough to strategize about the situation. Confronting your partner and gently letting them know that their rants are taking a toll on you energetically may be in order.

Emotional Intelligence and Earth Angels

Emotional intelligence has become so popular a concept that some companies even test new recruits and potential managers on their level of emotional intelligence. People who are highly sensitive and empathic, like earth angels, may be more likely to have a naturally high level of emotional intelligence. Emotionally intelligent people are very aware and mindful of their own emotional states as well as the emotional states of others. Because of this, the emotionally intelligent person may be more responsive to other people's emotional states. Emotionally intelligent people might be great at intellectual pursuits, but they are also smart about feelings.

Earth angels are often good at reading people and feel in a clairsentient way what is really going on behind the smile or frown someone is wearing in the world. The emotionally intelligent person might sense that someone smiling at a baby shower is actually crying inside because they've had trouble conceiving or adopting and might welcome someone engaging them in a conversation about anything other than babies. The emotionally intelligent person might realize that someone else's frown or gruffness at an after-work drinks outing is actually just shyness and that this person needs more encouragement to feel safe opening up socially. In offices, the emotionally intelligent coworker might be the person who is quick to pick up on everyone's quirks and triggers. Emotionally intelligent people are good at managing others, able to adapt their demeanor or approach to suit each individual, and sometimes become known as the office diplomat or mother/father.

Emotional Intelligence in Earth Angel Action

In my mid-twenties, a friend and I were out for coffee. My friend started telling me about a big fight he'd just had with one of his oldest childhood friends, "Bill," who had recently moved to town. I barely knew Bill, but it's always sad to hear about old friends falling out. The next weekend, that same friend had a big party, and Bill showed up. When Bill walked into the main room where the party was happening, I sensed he felt vulnerable and uncomfortable being at a party thrown by someone he was not currently on the best terms with. I also knew he didn't know many people since he had just moved. I had met Bill briefly years before, so without thinking—or perhaps not thinking with my brain but with my empathic sense—I walked over to Bill and made a big show of saying hello to him. Giving him a hug, I told him how nice it was to see him and chatted with him for ten or so minutes about his move and how he was settling in.

Bill's energy instantly changed as I called his name and crossed the room to greet him, and a beautiful smile spread across his face. I remember it made me feel so good to have his energy change to one of openness and ease, and I recall recognizing that I had come to say hello to him not because I particularly wanted to but because I knew it would be beneficial for him. Of course I was not acting entirely selflessly, because those feel-good vibes you get from making someone else feel good are an incredible buzz.

My friend who was throwing the party came over to me later and said, "I saw what you did for Bill. That was really sweet." Then he went on, and as only a good friend can do, told me something about myself that, at the time, I had not yet realized. "Tanya, you are so good at making people feel at ease. You always seek out the person who is feeling out of place or upset and try to make them feel better." My friend was trying to tell me I was an emotionally intelligent earth angel, and his insightful and complimentary comments were a true sign of his own emotional intelligence.

Learning Emotional Intelligence

If you have a partner or employee or child who isn't naturally emotionally intelligent, it can be learned—just like we can learn to read or speak a foreign language. For example, John Elder Robison is a memoirist who has written of his experiences with Asperger's. While everyone's experience with Asperger syndrome is different, many experience some degree of challenge with social interaction and nonverbal communication. While Robison may not be naturally emotionally intelligent, he is a kind, sweet man who happens to be a whiz with science, electronics, cars, and engineering. Yet he finds interpersonal relationships challenging. There are many funny anecdotes in his memoir, but one of my favorites is when Robison begins working at an office and is dumbfounded by the notion of small talk; he hated it, believing it was totally unnecessary. However, he gleaned that small talk was important to his coworkers, so he trained himself to engage in it and mimic the emotional cues of frustration or happiness he saw in his colleagues.

While earth angels can be drawn to any career, their emotional intelligence is one reason they might find themselves in careers where they work closely with people, like being an interviewer, a teacher, a counselor, or a manager. You might even find yourself in a career where you are teaching people emotional intelligence.

What leads to emotional intelligence? Partly it's being in touch with your own emotions. This means recognizing, honoring, and processing your emotions. That requires awareness and allocating space in your life for you to experience your emotions. Teaching people to value the emotional experiences of others—even if it appears contradictory or inconvenient—can help foster emotional intelligence. The next time someone wants to tell you how they feel about something, simply listen. It is simple yet powerful. This is a technique that the astute Robison quickly picked up on in his new office environment—people just want to be listened to. Listening to someone else's emotional experience can be very validating to the other person in and of itself, and it's a sign of your own exceptional emotional intelligence.

People Pleasing and Codependency

Emotionally intelligent earth angels might be well-liked professionally or socially, but they can also easily fall into people-pleasing behavior. If you're an earth angel, make sure you know who you are and what you want, as well as being good at knowing others. Pay as much or more attention to your own quirks and triggers as you do to the quirks and triggers of those around you. If we don't keep grounded in our own energy and keep coming back to ourselves at different times throughout the day to ask, "What do I need right now?" we can easily be pulled into too many other people's energy and lose our center.

Earth angels may enjoy getting lost in other people's problems, drama, needs, or feelings because it's a convenient way to escape their own issues. If you're an earth angel and are avoiding dealing with an issue in your romantic partnership, health, or finances, be aware that you could more easily fall into codependency as a way to put off taking care of yourself. Codependency is a way for an individual to focus more on someone else, and the other person's emotional needs become your own. In codependency, you may believe that without someone else feeling okay, you cannot feel okay. Don't be afraid to look at an issue in your life—like codependency—just because you don't immediately know how to handle it. Your intuition, your divine angels, and help from loved ones and professionals will assist you in figuring out how to handle something once you are willing to look at it. There are many resources and books about codependency.

As a very emotionally intelligent child, I was not the kid you wanted to make captain of a sports team, because I would pick the kids who were bad at sports and never normally got picked—those types of decisions were emotional, not practical ones for me. That's something for earth angels to be mindful of when making decisions about their finances, relationships, or self-care—use your heart (emotional intelligence) *but* also consult your head and your intuition. In the example of picking kids for teams, it might have been better for me to pick an equal amount of kids with my head (good at sports) as those I picked with my heart (kids who needed to feel included). With this formula, we would have had a well-balanced team that had a shot at winning or at least performing in a way that would raise my more vulnerable teammates' confidence levels.

Earth Angel Adaptability versus Shape-Shifting and Morphing

Earth angels might hear others say things about them such as, "You get along with everyone." Do people say you're easy to talk to or that you seem to see the best in people? Because earth angels are so empathic, it can be natural for them to get along with people of all walks of life. Being adaptable is a gift. You can tune in to others and get on their wavelength or see where they are coming from and have the ability to mirror it back to them or get in touch with the part of yourself that can relate to another and amplify it.

After having so many sensitive clients (and several close sensitive friends) I have repeatedly heard sensitive people express some level of concern about this amazing adaptability. You might find yourself being an entirely different person with different people. "Who is the authentic me?" you could occasionally ask.

All of us are complex beings with many different sides to ourselves that can be expressed in a healthy way, and sometimes these aspects can oppose each other. You might love to blare hard rock and dance around the house some days, and other days you cannot imagine anything but listening to nature sounds and curling up with a good book. Where sensitive people get into trouble is doing things that aren't authentic just to fit in or doing things that are actually self-sabotaging to better relate to another or make them feel comfortable. Earth angels especially want to make others more comfortable or feel good.

For example, a sensitive earth angel might be looking for a part-time job during college and find an organic bakery to work at. Most of the people working there are athletes at the college. Being around these coworkers, the earth angel gets into the side of herself that loves grounding into her body and doing physical activities. It helps her bond with her coworkers and is healthy. Where this earth angel might get into trouble is when she starts working out with the athletes after her shift at the bakery every day when she senses they would love to have her around, when *she* would really love to be in her dorm room drawing instead. Or she might get into trouble offering to load big bags of flour into the bakery to be one of the gang and help out when she does not have the upper body strength to do so safely. Sensitive earth angels may not realize they have shifted from healthy adaptability to unhealthy morphing until the line has been crossed in a significant way.

Adaptability is a highly desirable trait, but earth angels should not feel as though they must be all things to all people. If you are an introverted earth angel who is on vacation with a very extroverted friend, you might enjoy doing *some* of your friend's suggested activities, like dancing together at a club all night or going on an all-day snorkeling tour with a bunch of strangers. You might initially fear these things are too far out of your comfort zone but then be very glad you experimented with the boundaries. Yet, you will also have moments on this vacation where you have to pull back and honor yourself, like telling your friend you need a quiet afternoon with low stimulation like reading silently together at a café or maybe even a few hours completely alone sitting on the balcony of your hotel room.

When sensitive people find themselves morphing or shape-shifting to please others—like a parent who is trying to be all things to their children—it can become a self-sabotaging pattern. Over time, morphing behavior can cause an earth angel to forget who they really are and what really makes them happy. Remember that at the soul level, we were all made unique for a reason; when we forget who we are it is not good for us or the world.

There is a wonderful movie by the late Dr. Wayne Dyer called *The Shift*, wherein a character goes on vacation with her family and slowly realizes that she has spent many years shape-shifting and morphing into what her family—in this case her husband and young children—wanted from her. At the end of the vacation (and a mini-breakdown), she sends her family home without her. As she sketches a nature scene and rediscovers the artistic pursuits she used to love, she lovingly explains to her family that she needs one more week on retreat by herself to reground into her own energy and what she wants as an individual.

Have You Always Been Sensitive but Didn't Know It?

After reading this chapter you might feel as though things that never made sense before about you or how you interact with the world suddenly make perfect sense. It happens regularly in sessions with clients whom I pick up intuitively as being incredibly sensitive that they will tell me they are not at all familiar with the concept of sensitivity. I think it's a shame that naturally sensitive people go through life without this important information about themselves, so if you know someone who is sensitive, be a good earth angel and enlighten them about their sensitivity. There are so many sensitive people on the planet, and even more suddenly opening to new levels of sensitivity that there is no need for secrecy. If you know sensitive children, ask their parents or guardians if it would be acceptable for you, together, to find a way to word information about this child's sensitivity to them in a way that is helpful, comforting, and empowering. Don't push anyone—simply open the door and see who'd like to walk through.

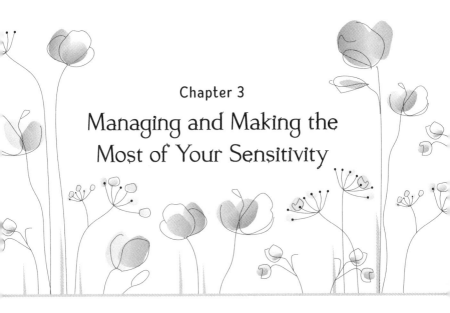

Chapter 3

Managing and Making the Most of Your Sensitivity

In this chapter we'll discuss how to better navigate life with your sensitivity, explore some of the gifts and challenges being very sensitive can pose, as well as how your sensitivity is affected by forces in the world outside yourself. There are things you need to watch out for and avoid as a sensitive person, and things you should definitely embrace and do on a regular basis to manage, engage, and make the most of your sensitivity. Think of your sensitivity like a comic-book hero's superpower. When the superhero initially discovers their unique ability, they go through a period of learning how to hone this skill and manage their exceptional power. I hope this section of the book helps you do the same.

Recognizing and Managing Overstimulation

The following might be signs that an earth angel's very sensitive system is overstimulated:

- Racing thoughts
- Free-floating anxiety
- Physical or mental exhaustion
- Having over-the-top emotional reactions
- Inability to cope with minor stressors
- Trouble concentrating
- Daydreaming about getting some alone time
- Resentment
- Being short or snappy with people you care about
- Not being able to bounce back from a busy day or week

These might also be signs of something else, so check your diet, make sure you are taking your supplements/medication regularly, or make an appointment with your health-care provider to run some tests to see if all is well with you physically.

When you realize you are overstimulated, build in some retreat and recovery time, which might look like one or any of the following:

- Spending a quiet evening in.
- Letting your partner, roommate, or children know that you're a little exhausted so you need the house to be a calm, drama-free zone with good, gentle vibes for a bit.
- Closing the door to your office.

- Leaving the office on your lunch break.
- Putting on some soft music.
- Getting lost in a fun, stress-free hobby.
- Getting a massage.
- Attending a gentle yoga class.
- Taking yourself out for a date alone.
- Grabbing a nap.
- Saying "no" to things and people who can wait.
- Reading a good book.
- Indulging in a soak in the tub.
- Putting off any work or phone calls or confrontations that can wait a day.
- Putting off thinking about any upsetting issues that can wait a day.
- Spending time outside.
- Cuddling up with a child, pet, or partner.

What Causes Earth Angels to Become Overstimulated?

Part of being overstimulated is a technical issue with your sensitive nervous system. Since earth angels are hyper perceptive and pick up more easily on subtle stimuli, being overstimulated simply means you have picked up on so much that your nervous system cannot comfortably process it all. If you have had a very busy week at work, you were picking up on all the noises and sights and smells and conversations in the office, all the work on projects you were involved in, and also some of the energy and emotions both individually and collectively of your coworkers.

Imagine that your nervous system is a physical container for stimulation. Thinking of your nervous system as a pitcher, being overstimulated means there is more liquid in the pitcher than it can hold. The solution? Stop pouring more water into the pitcher. In other words, stop exposing your nervous system to new stimulation and asking it to process that stimulation when it is overwhelmed trying to process the stimulation you exposed it to already.

As far as how much stimulation you can comfortably handle as a sensitive earth angel, some of this will be down to individual preference and limits as well as building up a tolerance. If you have a home bustling with kids and their activities, you will naturally begin to build up a tolerance to higher levels or amounts of stimulation. Yet when the kids go away to college and it's just you and the lazy dog left at home, over time you might lose your tolerance to so much stimulation, so that when everyone comes home for the holidays you feel a bit frazzled rather quickly.

You'll get used to recognizing the different stimulation levels of different situations. Attending an outdoor concert of one of your favorite rock bands with a new friend you can't wait to get to know and bond with during the show has a much higher stimulation level than sitting on the porch with a glass of wine alone while catching up on the new season of your favorite show. Both activities are very pleasurable, but do you see how one is much more stimulating than the other to your nervous system?

Earth angels tend to show up for everyone else and can put themselves on the back burner. So when you find yourself feeling frazzled, look back on the past week or month and see how much of your energy has been going outward versus how much has been focused on yourself.

Perhaps part of your retreat and recovery time when you realize you are overstimulated will be sitting quietly with a journal and seeing if there is anything upsetting you that needs your attention. Maybe you have been stressed about finances and stuffing down the fear because you don't want to bother anyone else with your problems, or perhaps your partner said something cruel or didn't support you in a way you expected and you need to confront them. Denying or avoiding your emotions can be much more stimulating, in a bad way, than facing them.

Negative or challenging emotions and circumstances should not frighten earth angels. Given their tendency to see the cup half full and be naturally hopeful, earth angels might shy away from negative emotions or pretend that a situation isn't as challenging as it seems. The earth angel's nervous and energetic systems are also sensitive, so they might believe these challenging emotions or situations will overwhelm them. Yet if you make some time to recognize and process these emotions, they can actually move through you much quicker instead of getting stuck in your system. Challenging situations will feel more manageable to you when you address them and start to slowly make progress.

Remember, if you are ever trying to work through a challenging emotion or traumatic experience and you feel overwhelmed or unsafe, please reach out to friends and family or health-care professionals. Knowing that you don't have to process everything at once helps too. Go at a pace that works for you and your sensitive system. Always be gentle and nurture yourself along the way.

Healthy Retreat and Recovery Time versus Isolating

The feeling that you need to hide out or retreat for a long period because you are a sensitive earth angel is usually temporary and can happen for a few reasons. Maybe you recently found out about sensitivity, and articles written about this subject have explained so much about yourself. Once you realize that you have always been a little different, you may go through a protective phase where you want to guard yourself more around the world and others. Some of this instinct is an attempt to learn the rules of the game. You say to yourself, "I'm sensitive and I perceive more, so how do I protect myself from overstimulation and other people's energy?" The other thread to this initial retreat is the first realization of what sensitivity is and how it has affected you. It's common, upon this realization, to think back in time and try to nurture yourself for all the occasions you did not or could not protect your sensitivity in the past, of which there were likely many. So, if sensitivity is new to you, I think it's appropriate to hide out a bit initially, learn about sensitivity, and nurture yourself along the way.

Another reason people might want to retreat for longer than usual (as has been covered, it's normal for sensitive people to want to retreat a bit every day to recalibrate their systems) is because their sensitivity goes to a whole new level. In my late twenties, I became very ill and radically changed my diet to omit sugar, "bad" carbs, caffeine, alcohol, and so on. I had to be very strict with this diet, which came at the same time I experienced my Saturn return (an astrological phenomenon mentioned in the previous chapter). My sensitivity and intuition increased dramatically in a very short time frame, because being intuitive is part of my work in the world *and* I started what I now call the Third Eye diet.

It is often temporarily overwhelming and disorienting when your sensitivity suddenly increases. In fact, this discovery can keep people from wanting to find out more about their sensitivity or intuition, as if they will be opening up Pandora's box. Rest assured, however, that you will get used to this new level of sensitivity and so will your nervous system. If your feeling is that this hasn't been true for you, reach out to someone who is well-versed on intuition and sensitivity for guidance.

The third time when it might be helpful to retreat for an extended period is when something traumatic has happened, like the loss of a job or loved one, sustaining an injury or falling ill, or perhaps just the revelation of some shocking information about a family member, etc. This kind of big event requires any human to take some time to digest, but sensitive people will especially feel the need to retreat because it may take them longer to get their nervous and energetic systems to idle back into neutral, as their hyper-perceptivity will cause them to pick up on all the subtle stimuli around this situation, like other people's emotions about it. And if you happen to be a sensitive earth angel who is a spiritual seeker (I'm guessing if you are reading these words, you are), you will want time to digest and analyze this event from a spiritual perspective. You may ask yourself things such as, "Why did it happen, and what are the ramifications, lessons, and karma on a spiritual level?"

Any very stressful situation, especially an extended one such as an illness or sustained financial strain, has the potential to be taxing on your nervous system. When your nervous system is overwhelmed, it won't do well with extra stimulation. Retreating more regularly for a longer period may be a healthy option. Speak to a healthcare professional too.

While all sensitive people need to find regular times and ways to retreat, what we have been talking about in this section are those longer periods where you are not as out there in the world socially or maybe even professionally if you have some control over or flexibility with your work schedule. Author and psychic Sonia Choquette took months off her very busy schedule when she experienced three losses in a row—the death of her father, the death of her brother, and the end of her marriage—to walk the Camino de Santiago by herself. If you are working a nine-to-five job and feel the need to retreat after a major event or to help heal your burnout, you might make sure you get out of the office on your lunch break every day, chat less with coworkers, pass on volunteering for any new projects, and get out of the office on time every day. Sonia had to dramatically rearrange a very busy schedule planned out many months in advance that included international events and appearances. Spending a large chunk of time every day retreating, recovering, and reflecting was something she absolutely craved.

Beyond these milestones in life where we need to temporarily retreat on a larger scale, you should feel safe and confident walking around in the world with your sensitivity. Sensitive people often reach a level of self-awareness at some point in their lives where they understand they must balance between being out in the world and retreating more mindfully than others would in order to protect their systems from overstimulation. The balance will be different for everyone. You might factor into the equation how extroverted or introverted you are. Look back at times when your life felt very balanced, calm, and happy, and figure out what the ratio of retreat to being-out-in-the-world time was.

Some sensitive people can misread the balance and lean toward isolation. While on the surface this seems safer, you have to remember that the nervous and energetic systems enjoy being understimulated about as much as they like being overstimulated. It's true that in our modern culture, we are afraid of boredom, so it's healthy to look around sometimes and maybe just be bored. It means you are letting yourself be and not overscheduling your life. Wonderful breakthroughs in your personal life and career can be born out of boredom.

A very lonely and isolated feeling is different from boredom; it may be a sign that you need to get yourself out there more. Hanging out with friends, volunteering, signing up for a class, or even spending time with a pet can make you feel connected again. If you find something like social anxiety to be a problem or you have been feeling depressed and it is keeping you from connecting with others, don't be afraid to talk to someone about it, whether it's a loved one, a professional counselor, or a medical doctor.

The balancing act of how much time to spend out in the world versus retreating and recharging is a formula that will be different for each earth angel, and sometimes it won't be perfect. Just remember there may be times when circumstances or life events force you to reevaluate this formula and make adjustments.

Avoiding Overstimulation

We've talked already about how earth angels and other sensitive types need to find their sweet spot as far as how much stimulation is right for their systems. Again, we're looking for balance, and that balance can't always be perfect. We also talked about what to do when the nervous and energetic systems are overwhelmed with stimuli, and what the signs are when we're beyond our comfort zone. Remember that sometimes comfort zones are meant to be experimented with. You might think a certain job or volunteer role or creative project or social opportunity will be too much for you, and then after saying a hesitant yes realize it's just right or in time your system adjusts to this new level of stimulation. Don't be afraid to experiment.

Many sensitive and earth angel people I know are very aware of how much is on their plate at any one time, which is an excellent way to avoid overstimulation. Often people who are sensitive might like to have one weekend on and one weekend off with social engagements. Or if they have a busy Saturday seeing friends or running kids to birthday parties, they find it beneficial to spend Sunday on the couch, in the garden, or puttering around the house. This is the balance. The sensitive system registers more, so it needs more recovery time. People who are not as sensitive might have a weekend jam-packed with social events, flitting from one to the next from Friday night until Sunday evening. The balance, for them, is different.

Extroverts tend to be nourished by other people's energy, while introverts tend to be nourished by their own. Note that sensitive and earth angel people can be introverted, extroverted, or (like me) in the middle between the two. Wherever you fall on the introvert-extrovert spectrum will affect your system's threshold for stimulation as well.

One of the sensitive person's coping skills for managing sensitivity is managing their calendar. (Sensitive people are the type who are initially disappointed when a friend cancels but are secretly grateful to have the downtime.) Make sure there is a balance of stimulation with work, social, and family obligations and build in recovery time while also making sure you're not being too cautious and keeping yourself understimulated or isolated. If you are a sensitive person who has a tendency to isolate to manage your sensitivity but sometimes get the balance wrong in the favor of under-stimulation, consider joining a book group, volunteering at a school or with animals, making a regular date to meet a friend for dinner or coffee, taking a class that meets regularly, getting a pet, or even starting your own part-time business where you will be working with people.

Be mindful that it's not always possible to control your calendar. There will be certain days, weeks, or even months when you simply must be busier, more productive, or have more interaction with people at work or home. When you have a period that will be much busier than you prefer—like the weeks leading up to a big social event or to final exams—it's about recognizing that you are a sensitive person who is temporarily out of their sweet spot. The balance will be off, so your goal is to build in small bits of recovery time every day. This might look like leaving work during a busy deadline to get a half-hour pedicure or chair massage down the street, asking a coworker to take a walk in the park, or ducking out on your own to have a quick cup of decaf or tea at a café when the whole staff will be pulling a late night.

Forty-five minutes to an hour of downtime at night can work wonders. If you are a sensitive person and a busy parent, curl up with a good podcast or book for forty-five minutes after the kids go to bed. The sensitive person needs time alone to unwind and re-center. Make sure you give yourself this daily or as often as you can. I know this can be a real challenge with parents, especially when the kids are young. Get creative with daily ways you might build in small recovery time moments (even fifteen minutes), and then make it a weekly goal to get one or two longer recovery periods.

Another option is to write yourself a mental IOU. If I have a busy week with clients, I will write myself a mental IOU that at the end, I will take myself to a restaurant for lunch alone or go to my favorite outdoor café and write all day. It's important during a busy week of interacting with people to know that in a few days

I have some low-stimulation time to look forward to. You might have something similarly calming that you can get lost in—a creative pursuit, or perhaps a project around the house.

Another highly sensitive friend and I were talking about how we like to block out two days in the week that are not necessarily back to back. If you work at an office, you might ask your boss if there is a day in the middle of the week or even an afternoon you could work from home. This allows sensitive people to have a break from the energy of others in the workplace and they often find they get more done at home.

Here are some tips for avoiding overstimulation:

Create a healthy routine. Routine is very calming to the nervous system. A healthy routine might look like waking up and going to bed at the same time every day (this helps your circadian rhythm), taking the same yoga class every week, or taking a walk through the neighborhood with your partner or pet after work.

Bring balance. The more areas of your life you can bring into balance, the less stressed your nervous system will be. When one area of your life comes into balance—such as eating habits or your spending habits—it can have a healing holistic effect on other areas of your life.

Develop healthy discipline. Enforce some rules you know will be good for you even if you don't like them in the moment, in the same way your parents used to enforce a reasonable bedtime when you were little. Indulge in substances like alcohol mindfully, or maybe you find that abstinence is a better route for you. Look for the long-term instead of short-term payoffs. Eventually you will begin to crave healthy discipline.

Keep your surroundings tidy. Do you find you are less stressed if you go to bed with and wake up to a clean and organized house? Because your sensitive nervous and energetic systems pick up on everything, a sink perpetually full of dishes or piles of laundry that sit on the couch for days can be even more distracting for you, as can a messy desk or overstuffed file cabinets. If you enjoy energy clearing, you can help clear the room with aromatherapy spray, the sound of a bell, or the burning of incense after you tidy. As a sensitive person, you might notice a significant energetic difference in the room afterward, like your nervous system feels more relaxed.

Stay on top of things. If bills or chores or deadlines at work aren't taken care of in a timely manner, it can be very taxing on the nervous system. Try to make a little progress every day or week toward meeting your obligations. Sensitive people are often comfortable with a slow and steady rhythm.

Make your self-care sacred. We will spend a whole chapter on self-care later in the book, but I wanted to emphasize here how much self-care protects and nourishes the sensitive nervous and energetic systems. Self-care also helps you stay grounded in your own energy, an important yet sometimes challenging thing for earth angels.

Earth Angels and Emotional Honesty

Being an earth angel definitely has its shadow or challenging aspects. While earth angels came here to be of special service to others, their mission can cause them to feel very un-earth-angel-like at times unless they practice great self-care and learn to put themselves first. One of the components of that self-care is putting yourself first by practicing emotional honesty.

I find that when I am writing about a particular subject for a book or article or working through a pattern or block in my life, the universe will lovingly send me examples of that subject or pattern. While writing this book, I had a session with an earth angel client. "Lexy" had become the unofficial "office mom"; she always worried about her coworkers and managers and worked actively to make sure the office environment was friendly, warm, and uplifting—not toxic. None of these duties were related to her job, mind you. Her job title was something completely different, not even close to the nurturing, mothering energy she brought to the team.

The pattern of being very reflective and concerned about the emotional experience of people in her office was directly linked to Lexy's sensitivity and mission as an earth angel to support others, a pattern that extended into her personal life as well. Lexy had a good friend who had the habit of doing something that always hurt Lexy's feelings. This situation did not happen often but it happened often enough that it was becoming an issue. I suggested to Lexy that she diplomatically and lovingly tell her friend that what they were doing was hurting Lexy's feelings. Due to her earth angel sensitivity, Lexy's first reaction was concern for and anticipation of her friend's feelings: "I haven't said anything up until now because I don't want to upset them." I pointed out that there was a pattern for Lexy at home and work: considering the emotional needs of others and putting her own on the back burner. This pattern prevented Lexy from being emotionally honest with others, which sometimes even kept her from being emotionally honest with herself.

"I know your friend does not mean to hurt your feelings," I explained, "but everyone is entitled to their own emotional experience. What your friend is doing hurts your feelings. That's valid and needs to be addressed."

"But if I tell her, the only thing I will be accomplishing is honoring my own emotional experience," Lexy said in a dismissive tone, as if honoring her own emotions was a small and trivial thing.

Like Lexy, perhaps you know that it's important for all of us to pick our battles with others in our lives. We don't want to create unnecessary drama—which can be taxing to the earth angel's sensitive or hyper-perceptive system—by sharing our every emotional reaction. However, when we don't share important feelings in an honest way to the important people at the important moments, we might not be living up to our role as earth angels. Earth angels came here to help others, and sometimes the way we help the people in our lives is through tough love, although I think we can always add a spoonful of sugar to tough love's medicine.

Honor your own emotions honestly by first asking: "How do I feel in this current situation?" or "What do I need from this relationship right now?" When you do this, you do so much more than honor or bow to your emotions; you open the doorway to increased intimacy and honesty with yourself and others. As a result, people feel free opening up about what does not work for *them* in their relationship with you.

Tuning In and Out

If we honor one emotion, our psyches might feel safe or empowered enough to share other information with us, such as something in our diet, at our job, or in our love life that isn't working for us and needs to be felt, examined, and shifted. Part of earth angels being in touch with their emotions is not letting all their energy go outward. A common question I get from clients who are sensitive is, "How do I block out some of the information I am receiving about others so I don't withdraw, isolate, or feel afraid of being out in the world in a larger way?"

When you are sensitive, it's natural to receive information. Tuning in to someone else with your feelers is a wonderful way to find out how others are, and be of more service to the people you interact with. However, when you are tuning in to another person, all your energy is directed outward. We humans need to have a fair amount of our energy also directed inward or focused on ourselves and our own journey.

If you are sensitive and go to a big party, it might be really fun to meet new people and tune in to them or have heart-to-hearts with old friends. You might find that tuning in is just second nature. But recognizing when you are tuned in, and learning to tune out mindfully, can become second nature as well.

Some sensitive people might feel like they do not have much control over the amount they pick up from others. I wonder if for some of them developing a tougher outer layer simply by placing themselves *occasionally* in situations that are apt to make them pick up a lot—like a busy grocery store—can help. As a fellow sensitive, this method has helped me. Experimentation is key, as is remembering that everyone is unique.

After a big social or professional event or going deep with some old friends, it will probably feel good to spend the next day focused on your own self-care or quiet time with your family or roommates where everyone does their own thing. In other words, schedule in that quiet downtime where your energy system has some space to stretch out, power down, and breathe.

Earth angels who work in large, open-area offices, teach in classrooms, or hustle around a hospital might have to be mindful of how much they tune in to other people. There is a difference between talking to someone casually or gathering practical information from them and tuning in to their energy and emotions intensely. It's all about focus. Throughout the day, check in and ask yourself where your focus is. If a coworker tells you they lack self-confidence sometimes at work, are you spending the next hour in the back of your mind wondering how you can pep talk them or prove their worth to them? If a client or patient went through a bad breakup a few weeks ago and is obviously still hurting, do you find yourself at home in the evening worrying about them?

When I'm on a call as an intuitive, I am with a client 110 percent during that call. They have all my attention, focus, and heart. But when the call is over, I hang up the phone, jot down my notes about the session for the client's file, and then take my mind immediately somewhere else. If an intuitive hit about the client floats in after the session and I believe it is significant, I will email them the information. And if someone is having a very rough time, it's natural that they might cross my mind over the next few days. When that happens, I say a quick prayer for them and then let the thought go. Because I read for hundreds of different people every year, I would not last in this job more than a week if I were unable to tune in to and then out of people at will.

So if the idea of tuning in and out at will sounds intimidating, I'm living proof it is possible. If I can do it working with so many people on such an intimate level, I know you can too.

Something that helps me tune in and out of people is self-care. One of my favorite spiritual teachers, Robert Ohotto, explains that one of the best energy shields you can have is good self-care. When you are frazzled and run-down, it's much easier to get pulled into someone else's energy. Good self-care grounds you into your own energy, which helps prevent getting randomly pulled into other people's. If you traditionally have problems tuning other people out, try improving your self-care even more. Also try grounding into your own energy by doing anything where the focus is on you, like meditating or even giving yourself a facial.

Develop a Meditation Practice

Meditation is a tool of presence that will come more naturally to you the more you practice it and increase feelings of calm and decrease anxiety. If you already have a meditation practice, it will go a long way to stop you from tuning in to others when you don't want to. Meditation helps train the mind, and learning to tune in and out of other people's energy mindfully is about training as well. In *Getting in the Gap*, author Wayne Dyer described meditation as increasing the space between your thoughts. In this way you are simply creating less unnecessary noise in your mind.

Some people do well with traditional meditation, or getting into a relaxed position and practicing making the mind still. If this works well for you, you might do this once or twice a day to calm your nervous system and reground into your own energy. If this type of meditation hasn't worked for you or feels intimidating, there are other ways you can create more space between your thoughts.

For many people, an active body encourages the mind to be still. Yoga, walking, or simply doing the dishes might encourage your mind to quiet down. You might find that listening to calming music or nature sounds helps your mind be peaceful.

Play games with yourself to help train your mind to be still. For example, try to meditate while grocery shopping: try to decrease your thoughts and create more quiet space in between them while you are shopping...not necessarily assuming the lotus position in the middle of the soup aisle.

Earth Angel Exercise
Tuning Out of Someone Else's Energy
This is an exercise that in theory can be done anytime and anywhere. You'll have to make modifications depending upon if you are in a roomful of people or alone.

Step 1. Identify the person or energy you want to tune out of.
You might be in a meeting and realize it is really the energy of an overbearing manager you want to tune out of or a colleague who appears bored or sleepy. In a large grocery store at a high traffic time, it might be the general energy of hustle and anxiety you want to tune out. If you are at home alone, identify the person you're thinking about who is causing distress, like the sibling you just spoke to supportively on the phone who is feeling down.

Step 2. Focus on something else.

In the case of the meeting, focus on someone in the room whose energy you either like or feels neutral. You might find an object in the room to focus on like a poster or painting. You could go inside if the meeting is not vital and do some visualization exercises where you picture a healing golden light starting at your heart center and slowing growing outward. In the supermarket example, don't focus on the anxious people around you, but on all the options in the snack aisle, or the gorgeous colors of produce, or the baby in the cart in front of you who is smiling and waving your way. You can also go inside in this scenario and focus on your own calm, rhythmic breathing. In the case of the sibling who is on the other side of the country and upset, focus on anything else that is peaceful or neutral and can occupy your attention—a good book to read, a tv show to watch, a child to play with, a pet to snuggle, a meal to cook, an exercise regimen to follow, a guided meditation to practice.

Step 3. Every time your mind goes back to the person or situation you want to tune out of, remind yourself to focus on something else.

The way we tune in to someone else's energy is by thinking of them, paying attention to them, or focusing on them in any way. Let's take an extreme example: You're on a plane and as soon as the pilot announces the descent, a toddler behind you starts wailing. It's a deafening and emotionally unsettling sound that becomes rhythmic as the toddler screams "no!" over and over. Other passengers around you start turning to look and showing signs of irritation. The poor parent is doing everything they can to soothe this child whose ears are being affected by the altitude change, but nothing is working. The child's screaming is getting to you big time because you're more sensitive to physical stimuli, and your sympathy is going out to everyone as a sensitive person. The seatbelt light is on and no one can escape. How do you focus on something else? Possibilities include: putting on headphones and playing some gentle music; rubbing your arm and concentrating on the feel of your skin or the texture of your shirt; saying a mantra in your mind like, "We'll be out of here soon and all will be well"; doing some deep breathing exercises and focusing on that; ignoring the reactions of the other passengers by looking at your book instead of all around you; calling on an archangel like Chamuel to help you keep the energy directly around you calm; or even trying to positively send calm energy to others. It's all about what you focus on. You won't be able to completely switch your focus in this kind of extreme situation; know that what connects you to anyone or anything is mostly what has your focus. For sensitive people, it is valuable to have clear distinctions of what can and cannot be controlled.

Getting Caught Up in the Challenging Energy of Other People Does Not Help Anyone

Sometimes sensitive people try to control the emotional energy of a family, office, or other environment made up of several personalities because they simply sense the collective energy is toxic or not warm and fuzzy. While we can pick up on other people's energy secondhand in the same way someone might walk into a room and smell something funny, remember that this activity is still largely a matter of focus. Keep bringing yourself back to what you need today, what your issues are, how you are feeling in the moment. In other words, keep bringing yourself back to your own energy. This is great to practice at a large family gathering like a holiday or other celebration. You will be given plenty of chances to refrain from codependently managing and tracking everyone else's emotions and instead have the freedom to focus on creating a nurturing bubble for yourself. Is Uncle Ted acting out and Aunt Alice being controlling? That's a great time to take one of your small cousins outside to play or make an excuse to run to the store for supplies. You don't have to feel everyone's emotions and help them figure out how to manage things.

Your partner may be having a really challenging day at the office and texting you about it throughout the afternoon, but that does not mean you need to go on the roller coaster ride with them. Isn't it bad enough they are experiencing it? Maybe when you stop to focus on yourself, you realize that you are having an easy, breezy, wonderful day. Stay in that energy and experience. Focus on your partner tonight over dinner as you help them problem-solve and manage their own issues or call them for fifteen minutes on their lunchbreak.

Sometimes earth angels can attract people who have trouble managing their own emotional experience into their lives as friends, coworkers, or family members. These can be lovely folks and the relationships with them can become healthy and nourishing. But please put boundaries on how much you give to and help these souls with their emotional experience. People might learn best how to manage their emotions by watching your healthy example or not having someone else enable them so they have to figure it out on their own. You might have times when you make yourself unavailable to them, which can be healthy for both of you if you have become the person they always call when they are upset. Or you might redirect the conversation toward you and what is going on in your life to get their advice and take on things, again shifting the focus temporarily off of them.

If you find yourself emotionally giving a lot to a friend, coworker, or spouse, try steering them toward tools that will help them manage their emotions independently. This might be suggesting certain mind, body, and spirit or psychology books to read, a yoga or meditation practice, professional help, or just sharing with them anything that has worked for you regarding managing emotions. Then you can use that helpful earth angel energy somewhere else. Conserving your emotional energy in this way will help the other person *and* you to avoid earth angel burnout.

Are Energy Vampires a Thing?

Vampires are mythical creatures popular in ancient folklore and modern media. These beings are described as creatures that drain the life force of other people, usually by sucking out their blood. Have you ever been around a real-life human who you felt drained your life force? I'm sure parents of small children feel this way at times. Whether it's a demanding family member or a very vocal customer you just can't seem to please, we have all had situations where we feel emotionally and physically drained by another person.

A good way to know if you are being drained by someone else's energy is that you find them distracting. Sometimes being distracted by someone else's energy is a pleasant experience, like when falling in love. You find yourself daydreaming about your love when you are trying to concentrate on work, or find yourself having to read the same page in a novel over and over because you have been daydreaming about what you will say next time you see your crush.

However, we have all experienced those times when someone's energy is distracting and it feels terrible, like the micro-manager at work whose intense, perfectionistic energy can feel overbearing or the mother who is always worried about you and constantly shares her fears. These lovely people, who may not realize they are draining you or are energy vampires, are a great excuse to practice mindfully tuning in and out of someone else's energy.

There's a lot of information out there about energy vampires, so I will only take a moment to clarify how I use the term; specifically, it is not to make these people playing the role of vampire wrong or bad. Let's face it: I'm sure there have been times when we ourselves have been cast in the role of vampire and unwittingly drained someone else's energy. Speaking personally, I know I am an intense personality and can definitely imagine times when I have dominated a conversation, come on too strong with a romantic interest, or been so perfectionistic and paranoid at a job that I drove someone else absolutely nuts. So let's not make the subject of energy vampires an "us versus them" dynamic; I bet most of us have played the role of vampire *and* victim at some point.

If you find yourself in the role of victim, try not thinking about the person who is acting as vampire when they are not around. You can hold a crystal or create a protection field around yourself or cut an energy cord if that seems to help, but ultimately, thinking of someone strengthens our energy cord to them and is a way to tune in to them. Not thinking of the person is the strongest energy protection I know. It sounds simple, but as discussed with the example of the toddler screaming on the plane, it's not always easy.

When I think of a client before a reading, I am tuning in to them with my feelers. It's the most powerful way that I have of connecting with their energy—sometimes more powerful even than talking to the client, considering the kinds of things I can know about a client by thinking of them during my premeditation before I've even spoken to them in our first session together.

If you suspect someone might be acting as an energy vampire in your life—they make you feel extremely distracted, tired, or emotionally triggered—try not thinking about them unless you have to. Thinking about them when they are not around is almost as bad as when they are standing in front of you. If you are thinking about them or the situation in a productive way, such as trying to better understand your feelings or how to improve the relationship, that's one thing. But spinning your wheels ruminating on how much they annoy you is acting as vampire to your own energy.

When you are interacting with this person face-to-face or over the phone, try to keep your interactions brief and to the point. If a family member triggers you, say hello and briefly catch up with them at the next gathering and then mingle away. Try not to do anything to add to the drama of the situation, as unnecessary drama is a huge drain to your energy. To find out if something is unnecessary drama or drama you need to deal with, ask yourself how important this issue is to you. As an example, you may have experienced times when you had to bring up an issue or argue for something with your partner. These are battles or issues you probably would rather have not engaged in but were too important to your emotional or financial health to ignore. On the other hand, there might be something very important to you such as a cause you believe in, but getting in a social media battle about it with a friend is unnecessary drama. It might be better to have a chat in person or send a private message. Again, unnecessary drama is how you drain your own system.

If you find yourself playing blood—or rather energy—donor to someone playing the role of vampire, you can always try to ask them to modify their behavior. This may or may not work, or you may or may not even feel comfortable with this ask (like if the vampire is your direct manager). Remember that your power lies in your ability to control your own actions.

We each have our own energy shield generated by our own psyches/bodies/selves. You might imagine this shield like the force field around a spaceship in a science fiction movie that can repel attacks by other ships. Though it can be helpful at times to ask someone like Archangel Michael to come in and strengthen your shield, the more we take care of our own bodies and psyches the more power our natural batteries have to send to our shields. This is why someone who is really triggering at work may not bother you at all on a day when you feel rested, calm, and well fed, while that same person on another day when you are feeling less grounded and more frazzled can send you over the edge in a minute.

If modifying your own behavior does not work with an energy vampire, you may have to ask a close friend who knows the situation well or a health-care provider who knows you well for suggestions. Sometimes you might even have to consider removing yourself from the relationship or situation. Above all, don't be a victim, because while you may gain people's sympathy, ultimately you'll remain in the unhealthy situation.

Earth Angels Picking Up on World Energy

Up until now we have been talking about ways you can control tuning out of energy, but there is some energy you will pick up on and not have too much control over the matter. An example of this is world energy. It might be a positive world energy, like when something very healing happens on a large scale. Or it might be a very challenging world energy, like a natural disaster that devastates a country and claims many lives. You don't even have to know about the event (like watching news coverage) to possibly pick up on this energy. The *Star Wars* characters Obi-Wan and Yoda are able to sense a "disturbance in the Force" when something tragic happens on a large scale without being told any details of what has happened.

Another example of sensitive people being affected by world energy is the energy that moves through the earth in cycles, like the astrological energy that astrologers map and interpret. As an intuitive working with clients all over the world, I have noticed that there are energy cycles we all seem to feel and be similarly affected by. The only thing we are doing to participate in these energy cycles is be alive on earth during the time the cycle is moving through and affecting or activating folks.

Recently, I had a terrible nightmare and then went on Facebook the next morning and saw that a friend who lives on the other side of the country had just posted about having the worst nightmare she had experienced in a while. When I shared my dream with her, she said, "Good to know. Must be something in the air." You might have a week where you feel alive and wonderful and decide there is something in the air you are picking up on. A good example of this is when spring hits in the Northern Hemisphere. Not only does the weather get warmer, flowers bloom and people come out to socialize more. We are all also hit with the collective playful energy of romance, adventure, excitement, and new beginnings.

Being a Sensitive Earth Angel in the Digital Age

You probably have many ways that other people can connect with you instantly: messaging apps through social media, the text feature on your phone, email accounts, and so on. You might even be signed up to sites or news services that send you alerts when something's happening or changing in the world. Not only are these features at times physically exhausting, but for earth angels who are sensitive, they constantly pull you out of your energy and into the energy of others.

The reason that this digital era is especially triggering for earth angels is because earth angels so want to help others. Therefore when a loved one or client or colleague or student or patient sends you a message, the giver in you wants to immediately give them attention. Perhaps just to let this person know they are special and important to you, or perhaps you know this person does need some comfort or advice and you want to alleviate their suffering. Either way, the earth angel sees the opportunity to make someone else feel good, and therefore feel good themselves because they can serve. Thus earth angels will have the instinct to jump on the opportunity presented by a text or social media message or email. Every earth angel's life circumstances will be unique in this matter.

Even surfing around on social media can quickly pull you out of your own energy—a friend's comment about politics could be very triggering or her innocent post about hanging with her mom on Mother's Day when your mother is either passed away or not in your life for other reasons can bring you right into your friend's energy and out of your own (in a painful way). Yet social media is also a marvelous way to connect and keep up with friends. There are definitely pros and cons to the digital age, and navigating it as an earth angel involves coming up with your own rules, as long as those rules are not absolutes.

Occasionally when I tell sensitive people to watch how much news they consume, I've heard them reply, "I don't pay attention to the news or world events. I stopped years ago; it was too draining on my sensitivity." But we all need to know what is going on in the world, especially as living in a digital age means we are all connected and affected by each other more than ever. Sticking your head in the sand is not an ideal solution, so I encourage sensitive people to be mindful of their news consumption and how it's affecting them—yet stay informed somehow. As an earth angel you came here to help people in need. If someone is in need somewhere in the world—and many are in terrible need—it's important you know. Maybe there is nothing you can do directly. But staying informed allows you to make a difference in indirect ways like through your shopping habits and who you vote into office. Always prioritize your own mental and emotional health, though, when taking in news.

Take into account how your personal sensitivity reacts to these digital intrusions—some earth angels will have a much higher tolerance for it, perhaps because they are younger and have grown up in a digital world. Or you might work in a busy environment where there is a lot of stimulation and you've gotten used to blocking it out. Whatever your current situation and digital comfort zone, earth angels should honor their sensitivity by being mindful of how they interact with the digital world.

Remember that you are in control. Below are some tips for setting healthy boundaries.

Earth Angel Exercise
Honoring Sensitivity in a Digital Age

You'll know that you have become too immediately available to others and are being constantly pulled out of your own energy if the texts, emails, and alerts are making you feel frustrated, stressed, unable to concentrate, exhausted, triggered, or frazzled. When you are grounded in your own energy, you will usually feel peaceful, calm, and confident. Use the tips below to help you better navigate being a sensitive earth angel in an age of digital distractions.

Step 1: Rethink the alerts that let you know new messages from social media and email are waiting for you.

Often people will send each other messages through social media when the message is not urgent or time-sensitive. That ding or vibration on your phone letting you know a new Instagram or Facebook message arrived might be way more draining to your energy than you realize. Can FB messenger itself be an energy vampire? Absolutely. You can always let friends and family know that social media is fine to reach out with as long as it's not time-sensitive. Look at all your alerts this way, including the ones on your computer and phone for your email. Do you need the loud alert? Or can you check when it's convenient for you?

Step 2. Develop a new relationship with your phone.

Although they have enhanced our lives wonderfully, phones have also become social crutches, addictive ways to avoid being present, and excellent means of pulling us out of our energy. Are you happy with your ring tone, or would you rather have it on vibrate? When someone texts, do you scan the first sentence to make sure it's nothing urgent and then respond when you feel ready? When you are waiting for a friend or business associate to arrive for a lunch date or meeting, do you take the time to ground and center yourself, observe your environment, daydream, and maybe even meditate a bit? Or does your hand fly immediately to your phone? Your phone is not an extension of you, but many people feel as though it is, which is why they can completely lose it when they cannot locate their phone—myself included!

Step 3. Practice not being immediately available to people.

Get clear on who you do want to be immediately available to. And even among those people, you might let them know that during certain times of the day you just cannot be available unless it's an emergency. What issues do you have around being immediately available to others? If you feel the need to respond to every work email within seconds, get clear on whether this is something your boss expects or is it coming from a fear-based place like, "If I'm not always available every minute of the day, I might lose this deal." Is that a realistic fear? In some rare cases it might be, but for the most part it's not realistic. Sometimes waiting to respond to a friend or work contact until you actually have the space and time to do so in a relaxed, thoughtful manner will produce a higher quality or more authentic response.

Step 4. Watch where your energy goes.

If a text comes in from a friend who is upset but does not need an immediate response, are you able to notice the text and go back to what you were doing with the knowledge that you will respond later? If you are on social media and a friend's big, happy announcement about his promotion triggers feelings of hopelessness and jealousy, are you able to shake it off quickly and come back to your own energy? Simply being aware of your energy shifts and knowing you have a fair amount of control over them can help. You can acknowledge your challenging emotion *and* choose to put your focus elsewhere. Do something to engage your physical senses and ground back into your own energy when you become scattered, like have a healthy snack, put on some music, go for a walk, or dig into a project around the house or office.

Step 5. Notice any changes you experience after making tweaks to the way you interact with digital devices.

Remember this might be a case of trial and error, so you could unsubscribe from a newsletter to declutter your inbox and then realize it's something you miss and look forward to. Parents are usually mindful about their children's screen time. This is something sensitive adults need to be more mindful of as well. Less screen time and more mindful digital consumption with phones and social media could make you feel significantly more peaceful as it cuts down on the sensitive earth angel feeling overstimulated. In the past, life used to move a lot slower and be significantly simpler. (Maybe not better, but simpler.) The digital age is exciting and affords us all many wonderful opportunities to connect, yet earth angels need to be mindful of how much and at what speed things are coming into their energy field.

Earth Angels Giving and Receiving Criticism

The reason this section is within the chapter on sensitivity is because criticism can be very triggering for sensitive people. In my experience working with thousands of sensitive clients, many tend to be perfectionistic. Because a sensitive earth angel can easily pick up the energy and emotions of others, they have real skin in the game regarding not being exposed to criticism, since usually when people are critical they feel frustrated, angry, disappointed, and so on. If the sensitive earth angel is the recipient of the criticism, the accompanying emotions from the person doing the criticizing can be hard to sit with.

Sensitive people, like all humans, can tend to mirror the energy of others. This can be more true of the sensitive person, since they can pick up on other people's energy quickly and might catch themselves morphing or shape-shifting without realizing it, as covered earlier in this chapter. For this reason, the sensitive person could take on or mirror the intense emotion of the person being critical toward them, when a friend who is less sensitive would have shrugged the criticism off or taken it in stride.

"Ben" had just begun working full-time as an aesthetician. He'd completed his schooling but the center Ben was working at had him listed as someone who was just starting out, so his services were priced at a reduced rate. Initially nervous about embarking on this new career, Ben soon grew to love working with people one on one, sending his clients good vibes as well as offering them his compassionate ear while he worked on their skin. For this earth angel, it wasn't just about making people look good—it was also about making them feel good. Ben had always identified with being a healer and believed he was living that calling. One day, Ben received a negative review online for a service and was devastated. He questioned himself and his entire career choice, even though up until he had seen this negative review, he had always gotten very positive feedback.

As Ben and I talked it through, we were able to discern that the woman who'd written the negative review had difficult skin to work with, high expectations, and had booked Ben because of his lower rate without taking into account that he was just starting out as an aesthetician. Instead of feeling completely defeated and like an utter failure, Ben was suddenly able to see how this woman's own issues had played into the outcome. A sensitive earth angel, Ben was taking things too personally. Ben began to feel compassion for this woman who was frustrated by her challenging, sensitive skin.

Next, Ben and I looked—with compassion—at where Ben had played a part in the outcome. It's important for sensitive people to resist the urge to hide behind their sensitivity, such as saying, "I'm too sensitive to handle that level of criticism. It will crush me or I won't be able to bounce back." This particular client had asked for a certain treatment, and Ben had suspected that a different treatment would suit her skin better. The request made Ben feel uncomfortable—his training and intuition were telling him one thing, but the client was insisting on something else. Ben did what she wanted, so when she went home and did not like the results, she was upset and wrote a very negative review. Ben's takeaway was that he needed to get more coaching from some of the senior people at work. He would insist in the future on sharing his opinions more confidently with clients. Once Ben was able to look at the situation in a balanced way, he was able to take what was useful from the experience and leave the rest—the client's personal issues which he could never control—behind.

Sensitive earth angels should resist the urge to take ownership over someone else's challenging personal issues. Get clear on what someone else's challenging issues are, and remind yourself regularly that you have little or no control over this aspect of the relationship.

Ben also looked at the spiritual component of this interaction and decided that this client was spiritually teaching him to have a tougher skin. Working with the public, Ben was bound to occasionally come across people who would not like what he had to offer. He couldn't let negative experiences throw him off his game and make him question everything.

While taking criticism as a sensitive earth angel can be tough, it's often no easier to give it. As earth angels, we have to honor our deep desire to help others and be a positive force in the world, even when offering criticism to others...perhaps *especially* then. Being an author and knowing how much work goes into writing and publishing a book, I simply cannot bring myself to write a negative review of someone else's book. Yet I have benefitted and learned from reading negative reviews of my own books. And I know that offering criticism to loved ones or colleagues is important not only for their growth but also for my own desire to honor my emotions and perspective.

I used to question or reconsider my impulse to also be gentle, kind, or loving when giving criticism, but now I realize this is simply how I honor my earth angel energy. You might start out a discussion where you plan to offer criticism in the following ways: "I know you are trying your best"; "I appreciate you so much, but there's something I need you to work on"; "I don't think you are aware of it, but..."; "It's because I care about you so much that I have to say..." These are great things to open with when you are not in a heat-of-the-moment argument but are feeling calm and centered and ready to offer constructive criticism that can benefit both parties.

Earth angels are often known for being nonjudgmental. This does not mean they don't have strong opinions about social or world events, nor does it mean being a doormat. It simply means acknowledging that you have not walked in another person's shoes and that on a soul level, you are equal—even if this person has done something horrible. If you are offering criticism, try to wait until your emotions have cooled or do not feel so raw. Similarly, you do need to honor emotions such as anger (for example, when your boundaries have been crossed) by finding an appropriate time and way to communicate your criticism. As an earth angel trying to help others, you must realize that your criticism might be exactly what a person needs to hear to shift something important in their lives.

Earth Angel Exercise
Receiving, Surviving, and Using Criticism as a Sensitive Person

The following exercise involves looking at issues from the past in the hopes that some of the emotions around these issues have settled so that intense emotional reactions won't distort your viewpoint. Examining situations from the past to help you identify patterns and make shifts for the future is also beneficial because when we look at the past we have the benefit of hindsight and the wisdom it brings.

Step 1

Pick a situation from the past where you received criticism and it was painful and triggering, where you had a strong emotional reaction and turned on yourself because of someone else's criticism. Be nurturing with yourself now as you look back.

Step 2

Now identify any circumstances that were outside of your control, like someone else's issues. Perhaps a colleague came down hard on you for a mistake you made but now you realize this person was perfectionistic and had unreasonable expectations. Or maybe you were dealing with an illness at the time and simply were not able to perform at your best because of it.

Step 3

What was useful about the criticism you received? It might be something direct (such as doing something more efficiently), or more indirect (like your intense reaction to the criticism causing you to realize you were on edge and feeling run-down). Did it actually increase your self-love?

Step 4

Is there a spiritual takeaway? Can you see your colleague at the time as someone who taught you about working on your own perfectionism issues? Maybe seeing their issues forced you to come to terms with similar impulses inside you or made you realize that one of your parents had similar issues when raising you. Remember you can get clear on someone else's issues without making them a "bad" person.

Step 5

Did this trigger old wounds, like childhood trauma? When an old wound is triggered, sometimes the only way we realize it is the over-the-top reaction we have to the present. When this happens, be extra gentle with yourself and your inner child.

Step 6

How would you handle this situation differently if it happened today? Get clear on what you learned from the past so the next time you are criticized, you have different tools at your disposal to deal with the criticism. You might even create a protocol for when someone offers you direct criticism. If you tend to take criticism to heart, your protocol might look like calling a time-out so you can put some space around your emotions and let them cool down or talking to an objective third party about the situation before allowing yourself to take action. Above all, practice radical self-love.

Making Magic in Your Life and Making Your Sensitivity Work for You

An earth angel's sensitivity is a gift—one that every earth angel needs to help fulfill their collective mission in this life. While this sensitivity can lead your nervous and energetic systems to be more easily or quickly overwhelmed, it also gives you a ton of very useful information about the people and situations in your life. For example, you and your family might have just moved to a new state. After six months, you enjoy where you are living but are still settling in and feeling a bit disoriented. You really like it, but you're not sure if you can picture living there forever.

One night you and your partner are up late talking, sharing with each other how you are feeling about this new state. There is a sense of anxiety you both share—wanting to put down permanent roots and buy a home but not sure if the time or place is right. You have been renting but really want to own. This issue has been causing stress for you for weeks, maybe even months. "I might end up getting another job offer in a few years in a different state," your partner says at one point. As you discuss options—continuing to rent where you are, buying a home, or moving again—you hear yourself saying how hot the real estate market is in your new town and how it doesn't seem to be cooling down anytime soon. This is a fact you and your partner are well aware of.

"I think we should buy a house here in the next six months, and then if we want to move in a few years we can easily sell the house at a profit or rent it out," you suggest. "Then we don't have to feel like we are making a forever commitment to this area." It's a practical solution that seems to honor your desire to invest your money in a home, and also gives the flexibility to move from the area if your partner gets a better job offer in the next few years.

But more importantly, this solution *feels* right. As soon as you say it out loud and your partner agrees, you get a confirmation from your logical mind but also from a place more powerful—your soul. Your entire body relaxes. You feel light as opposed to tense, and even excited to execute your new plan. You will hear people say this all the time about a romantic partner or business opportunity: "It just felt right."

Sensitive people are naturally strong in clairsentience, the psychic pathway that allows one to feel information intuitively. You are the kind of person who can walk into an office on a job interview and feel it's the right place ... or the wrong place for you. Besides analyzing the salary, company, and position, you are also analyzing the vibes you are getting. A friend might have the feeling that a doctor you recommended is all wrong for her, yet for you the vibes are great and the health-care provider is a perfect fit. Keep in mind that the vibes each of us receives about the same people can be vastly different.

Learning to trust your feelings about people and situations is something sensitive people do to help them better navigate the world. Remember that your clairsentient feelings about a situation can be different from your emotions. You might feel really angry at your partner for something she said, but get the strong intuitive feeling that now is not the best time to confront her about this. If you listen to your intuition in this case, you can avoid, say, a big blow-up on the night of an important social event. You can still honor your anger and the information it is giving you—that your partner has crossed a boundary that needs to be addressed—but your intuition is simply telling you by putting out its feelers that now is not the best time.

You might be terrified to face some of your financial issues, and after you make an appointment with a financial planner or therapist to discuss the problems you are having, you get the intuitive feeling that this is right—something you just *have* to do. You might be scared all week leading up to the appointment and incredibly nervous as you go over your figures and concerns. Yet when you leave the office, you still get the intuitive feeling that while this process is difficult emotionally, it's absolutely the right thing to do. Perhaps when you get home you honor your fear by snuggling up with a pet or calling a good friend for a heart-to-heart or pep talk. Yet you make another appointment, because your sensitive feelers tell you it's right. Your emotions are reminding you that you have some fear and anxiety around this issue, which is also good to know.

Do you see how both your emotions and your intuitive feelers give you information, and both parts of yourself need to be honored? Sometimes when faced with two options that look equally attractive or sound on paper, the only thing we can go on is our feelers and the information they give us about which opportunity is better for us.

Our feelers or clairsentience is one way we can tap into a difference source of wisdom and knowledge. Having very sensitive feelers is a blessing, earth angel, and a way to help you better navigate and cocreate your life. And remember, you can also choose to put your feelers in or retract them slightly if you are overwhelmed, like when you're at a big conference or when a relative is in a lot of pain and venting to you. It's important to always ask yourself if putting your feelers out is serving you by giving you important feeling information, or is it simply distracting or draining you. If the answer is the latter, there are other ways to use your Spidey sense, like engaging witnessing energy.

Earth Angel Exercise
Retracting Your Feelers to Engage Witnessing Energy

Step 1

Pick a situation in your life to practice this technique on. It can be helpful to practice with a situation you are not too personally emotionally invested in. An example might be a challenging situation (not life or death) that is happening to a friend you care about, such as their romantic life or their career.

Step 2

Now let's approach this situation from the angle of retracting your feelers. Keep in mind you will still get a lot of intuitive information that might be helpful for your friend with your feelers retracted. In sessions with clients, I continually put my feelers out and retract them so that I get clairsentient information but do not become overwhelmed by it. I am also getting information from the other three clairs or psychic pathways—hearing intuitive guidance as a voice in my head (clairaudience), seeing images in my mind that give me intuitive guidance (clairvoyance), and knowing intuitive guidance as a breakthrough thought or download from heaven (claircognizance).

In some ways, I receive information by retracting my feelers and instead get into witnessing energy. Witnessing is grounding into your own energy with an objective, detached attitude and not tuning in to someone else or a situation with your feelers. Think of it like a clinical focus that pulls back for space, objectivity, and breathing room. It's the same way a doctor might focus very intensely on you while you describe your symptoms yet appear to have no emotional reaction to information that others might find emotionally unsettling.

When your witnessing energy is engaged, it'll feel like the energy is neutral, neither good or bad. You can picture this by imagining more space between your energetic body and the other person's, or visualize wrapping your energetic body around yourself tightly like a blanket. You'll know you have retracted your feelers when the other person's emotions do not produce a strong emotional reaction in you. From this vantage point, you might find yourself using your intuition to give practical advice, for example, as opposed to using your feelers to relay verbally that you understand exactly what the other person is going through.

Step 3

Now that you know you can use your sensitivity to tune in to a situation in two different ways—with your feelers or witnessing energy—practice mindfully using both off and on throughout the day. See how the energy differs with each technique—when you engage your feelers the energy will seem thick and with witnessing energy it will seem lighter. Make note of what types of situations are more suited to using your feelers and when you get a better outcome from engaging witnessing energy (a triggering person with an overbearing energy might be the perfect excuse to retract your feelers and employ witnessing techniques).

Working with Witnessing Energy

Most sensitive people can strengthen their witnessing energy. This does not mean you are cold or even have to appear cold to others. Let's say a dear friend comes over for lunch. As you sit on a bench in your garden, she tells you that something traumatic just happened to her sibling and begins crying. You naturally want to comfort your friend, so you may hold her hand (sometimes people just need you to listen) or tell her how sorry you are but remain in your own emotional skin.

This can be done by taking two steps back energetically and observing her by engaging witnessing energy. Think of it like watching a scene unfold on a city sidewalk as you pass by. Then, after you help reassure her and she leaves, say a prayer for her and take your mind somewhere else immediately. Get lost in a task or thinking about something you are struggling with. If any important intuitive hits are supposed to come to you about your friend's situation, they will naturally float to the surface over the course of the day as you place your mind somewhere else.

Putting out your feelers by feeling into a situation with your clairsentience is a powerful way to access knowledge and energy. And it's something that sensitive earth angels probably have a natural talent for or is a default setting in their wiring. The next time you are watching a movie where the characters' lives speak to you, notice how your feelers naturally come out so you can enjoy experiencing the highs and lows with these characters—and perhaps process some feelings about your own life in the process.

You might want to engage witnessing energy instead, especially if you are watching a documentary about something deeply traumatic or personally triggering for you. The way you engage with art—whether it's a painting, a poem, or a play—is the perfect place to practice extending or retracting your feelers. You will receive intuitive information either way.

When you go into witnessing energy, you may get intuitive information from any of the other three psychic pathways already covered: clairaudience, clairvoyance, or claircognizance. Out of the four psychic pathways, claircognizance (considered the intellectual psychic pathway) and clairsentience (the psychic pathway connected to feelers and feeling intuitive information) are the most common to experience. When you engage in witnessing energy, especially look for a breakthrough insight, an a-ha! thought, or a download from heaven.

Opening Up Completely to Your Sensitivity

This chapter has covered how you might protect yourself as a sensitive earth angel and how to manage your sensitivity, and it's just as important to open up completely to your sensitivity at times. I am reminded to do this almost every day whenever I am in a session with a client. People ask me, "How can you be a professional intuitive and walk down the street without getting overwhelmed?" The answer is I've learned how to manage my sensitivity. I know what it's like to focus completely on another person and also what it's like to ground into my own energy or avoid energetic distractions. It's never perfect but usually works!

With the right people at the right times, opening up to your sensitivity completely is amazing, such as when listening to one of your favorite bands at an outdoor concert on a cool summer evening or being physically intimate with someone you love, trust, and have beautiful chemistry with. You might be headed to a lunch date with a good friend and are so excited to see them you just want to be fully present with them—even every bit of your sensitivity.

I love to take walks in the park by my home, and in the spring it's covered in wildflowers of all varieties, shapes, and colors. Flowers are great teachers—showing us how beautiful and how fleeting earthly life is. I put on sacred, soothing music in my ear buds and wander through the park. I can feel my whole system open up, like the chakras on my palms tingling, partly because it is safe to do so.

Feeling safe is important when you want to open up completely to your sensitivity. Even in difficult times, you might decide you want to be completely open to an experience, because everyone around you is in a warm and compassionate place. You can open up to your sensitivity completely during everyday moments as well as peak experiences. If you ever feel overwhelmed opening completely, simply pull back and retreat for a time. The sensitive person might be the one at a festival or workshop who opts to spend one evening or a portion of every morning alone. Retreating for periodic recovery time will allow you to stay completely open more often.

It important to have times when you are completely open to your sensitivity because doing so makes you feel more alive, like you are getting every last drop out of life. Though we've talked about some of the shadow or challenging aspects of being a sensitive earth angel, the benefits far outweigh the challenges. When you are open to it, sensitivity allows you to really savor life, whether physical experiences like a great back massage or emotional experiences like bonding with a loved one.

Earth Angel Exercise
Opening Up Completely to Your Sensitivity

You might do this exercise when you will be spending time with people you are already comfortable with doing something either neutral (like a standard meeting at work) or pleasurable (like a picnic). You can also try this exercise when you are going into a situation that could be emotionally challenging. Or do this exercise alone, just like I do on my walks in the park.

Read the tips below a few times before going into any situation where you want to be open to your sensitivity. These tips will soon become second nature, easily called to mind when you want to be completely open.

- **Be present.** If you catch yourself thinking about your to-do list or worrying about an interaction you had with someone earlier in the day (sensitive earth angels are more prone to this) gently remind yourself to focus completely on the present moment. If you're with other people, open your posture and make regular eye contact.

- **Connect with your senses.** Is the room you are in warm or cold? If you're outside, what is the weather doing? Can you smell your coffee or the detergent from your shirt? How is your body liking the position you are in—is it comfortable? Notice any sounds or sights that stick out to you.

- **Breathe deeply.** Find a steady rhythm with your breath. Notice if it is shallow and quick or deep and even. If your breathing is relaxed it will help you slow down and pick up more with your sensitivity.

- **Focus.** Focus is one of the most powerful ways to open up your sensitivity and intuition. If you're having a conversation, focus on the other person and what they are saying. If you are out having a meal by yourself, focus on the food you are eating and how your body feels in the chair. If you're at a concert, focus on the music you are listening to and the performer on stage.

- **Notice any intuitive hits your sensitivity picks up.** These could come through any of the four psychic pathways covered: clairaudience, clairvoyance, claircognizance, or clairsentience.

- **Don't judge anything your sensitivity picks up on.** Just let everything register for now. You can examine, analyze, mentally catalogue, and sort through everything your sensitivity picked up on later. Your mind will naturally begin to reflect on the experience once it is over.

An Example of Rejecting or Embracing Your Sensitivity

I wanted to finish this chapter on sensitivity by looking at how embracing it can dramatically improve anyone's life. That said, sensitivity is such a huge part of an earth angel's experience that it will be brought up as a central theme throughout the rest of the book.

The 1987 film *Moonstruck* is considered a classic because the characters' lives and issues are so relatable, rich, and emotionally moving (it won three Oscars and was nominated for six). The lead character, Loretta (played by Cher), goes to the opera for the first time to see Puccini's *La Boheme*. She is skeptical about the experience and at intermission tells another character that she doesn't see what all the fuss is about. Yet she goes back to her seat to see the next act, and there is a powerful shot of Loretta crying during the opera, being incredibly moved by the stories of the characters on stage. We could say that her feelers have finally come out; until that point, Loretta had been closed off to her sensitivity due to a traumatic incident from her past prior to the events of the movie.

Loretta's emotional and energetic reaction at the opera is so powerful because it feels to her as if what is happening to a fictional character on stage is really happening to her. This is how empathy works—stretching your feelers allows you to empathize with others. In Loretta's case, even though she is crying and what is happening to the characters on stage is difficult, it is a pleasurable experience for her. She feels more and she feels more alive, and she knows the opera will end and she can go back to her real life soon.

If someone in Loretta's real life were dying, like the character on stage was dying, Loretta might have to be more mindful about how and when she stretches out her feelers so she would not be completely overwhelmed for a prolonged period of time. Loretta's stretching out her feelers and having such a moving experience at the opera allows her to be more emotionally open and available even after the performance ends, which gives her the courage to say yes to a love she's not sure can work out.

When we reject our sensitivity, what we're really rejecting is our heart energy, as the two are strongly connected. If you deny one, you begin to deny the other as well. In the beginning of

Moonstruck, Loretta is only making decisions from her head. She never allows herself to consult her heart. But after her emotional breakthrough at the opera (at the movie's halfway point), everything changes for Loretta because the place from which she is making her decisions changes. She's still practical and grounded *and* her heart now has a say in matters.

———

Use data from your feelers to help you navigate both big and small situations and create more magic in your life, knowing that you can also retract your feelers (especially if stretching them is draining). Go into witnessing energy where your emotions and energy feel neutral to gain information from your intuition in a different manner. Play and experiment with your sensitivity to know it and yourself better, and to create a richer, more heart-centered earth angel experience in this life.

Chapter 4

Earth Angel Burnout Symptoms and Antidotes

I believe that some element of burnout is a natural part of life. It's normal for us to take things too far, focus too much on one aspect of our lives, give too much, try too hard, let others push us beyond our healthy limits, and so on. Earth angels are not aiming for a perfect world in which they never experience symptoms of burnout. The goal is to catch the warning signs of burnout sooner rather than later, so that you don't end up with a tank on empty. In this chapter, we will be identifying signs of earth angel burnout as well as antidotes to each particular burnout symptom.

If you have been reading along in the book this far and haven't quite resonated with being an earth angel, or think you used to act and feel more like an earth angel in the past, you might be in burnout. Don't get angry with yourself if supporting others and holding an uplifting energy feels like the last thing you want to do—listen to that wisdom. If it *is* the last thing you want to do, make it so. Concentrate instead on healing your earth angel burnout. Some of the ways you do that will be by giving back.

Play a game with your intuition: ask for a number between one and twenty-three (to represent the twenty-three symptoms of burnout covered in this chapter). What number pops into your mind as a thought, image, or sound? Pay close attention to that symptom of burnout, because it's probably a factor in your life right now. You might be given guidance to pay attention to more than one of the numbered burnout symptoms in this section of the book.

Burnout Symptom 1:
Resenting How Much You Give to Others

You might start having resentful thoughts about how much more you do around the house than your partner or how much more time you put in at the office than your boss. Perhaps you find yourself venting to a friend over lunch about how a business partner is only a taker and never a giver. Resentment can be a very negative or toxic sensation, as if we have our head down and are marching unwillingly but with resignation through a snowstorm. On the bright side, feelings of resentment can be a great motivator. Sometimes challenging feelings act as powerful invitations to take action toward change.

Earth Angel Antidote

Resentment can be temporary, like having a bad day. But if you are experiencing consistent feelings of resentment about a relationship or situation in your life, take action. How can you change or renegotiate the dynamic? You'll know you have hit on a great solution when feelings of resentment begin to subside and you feel lighter, more empowered, and more in control. You should also feel more enthusiastic about giving to others and begin to take pleasure in giving again.

Burnout Symptom 2:
Focusing on Everyone but You

Do a little inventory now and again to see how many thoughts a day you spend on others as opposed to yourself. If a friend or loved one is really struggling, it's normal that they will be on your mind and in your thoughts more than normal. This can be equally true if something extraordinarily good is happening to someone else in your life, whether the circumstance makes you feel happy for them or suddenly upset and a bit jealous. Above all, be careful that you stay grounded in your own life and present in your own emotional skin. If you try to live all of the other person's pain or excited feelings with them, you will burn out—you have to simultaneously live your own life as well.

Earth Angel Antidote

Instead of being emotionally available or tuned in to someone 24/7, offer focused support. Limit the time you think about this person's issues to constructive chunks. If you are on the phone with them, let your heart go out to them and feel all the feelings. But when you hang up, slowly untangle yourself from their energy by doing another activity that requires your full attention, such as cooking a new dish or helping a child with their homework. Especially keep unnecessary or unproductive worry thoughts to a minimum. Remember that you are energetically connected to loved ones; remaining positive and hopeful about them could in some magical way help them to remain positive and hopeful as well. If seeing that an old high school friend is pregnant from a post shared on social media initially makes you happy for her but then disappointed for yourself, move away energetically and emotionally from your friend's experience and back into your own. This might look like counting your current blessings and acknowledging that we all have our own path and timeline.

Burnout Symptom 3:
Experiencing Emotional Overwhelm or Instability

I have a friend who loves to meditate and shared a priceless piece of wisdom with me a few years ago: "Sometimes we all just have a bad day. We might feel anxious or sad or overwhelmed, and then amazingly, the next day, it's totally different. We feel calm and positive and balanced. When I have a day where I'm feeling bad, it always helps to know that tomorrow could be a totally different experience." Emotions can be like the weather. Sometimes the clouds roll in and a thunderstorm follows, and then the following day is a moderate, sunny, and beautiful day with just the right amount of cool breeze. But if you have days or especially whole weeks in a row where managing your emotions feels impossible and being even-keeled seems like a distant memory, it could be a sign of burnout. Whatever is going on, make sure you get the help you need to feel better.

Earth Angel Antidote

If you are feeling emotional overwhelm or instability, make an appointment with your health-care provider to rule out any physical causes, like hormonal, thyroid, or vitamin and mineral imbalances—or any other physical issues. You might also consider taking a sabbatical from caffeine and sugar. Lean into your self-care. If you have been super busy and ignoring your body's dietary and sleep needs, pay more attention. Sometimes depression can make us ignore our daily self-care as well. Do a drama detox and avoid any unnecessary drama for a few weeks. Avoid triggering people and situations, take a break from social media and upsetting headlines, and monitor your negative or anxious thoughts. Initiate one calming routine every day, like gardening, cooking, reading uplifting books or articles, exercising, meditating, taking a long bath, chatting with a loved one who lives far away, or working on a project or hobby. Also try to treat yourself to a little fun. Earth angels can be very serious and might need a reminder to blow off steam. Mental health professionals are invaluable if you feel you have lost your emotional balance and cannot regain it on your own.

Burnout Symptom 4:
Lashing Out at Loved Ones

If you're an earth angel, it might be quite upsetting to find yourself blowing up at people in your life, as your modus operandi is to be warm and helpful. When we explode on someone, it can be a sign that our needs have not been met for a while. They have instead been suppressed and bubbling up under the surface and eventually spew out in ugly or destructive ways. Certainly you want to identify the underlying problem and modify your behavior if you are lashing out at people, whether it's loved ones or even strangers. It's just as important that you do not judge yourself for the behavior. Go into nurturing mode with yourself.

Earth Angel Antidote

If you're lashing out at people, call a time-out or a brief pause. When you are feeling calmer and more centered, sit down with a journal and ask your higher self—that wise part of you that is very observant and still connected very closely to Spirit—why you have been lashing out or exploding. Maybe there are some immediately understandable reasons. Maybe you need to try a different approach or tactic for getting your needs met. If you are overreacting or exploding on people when the situation does not call for it, investigate the underlying emotional issue. Are you upset about something else in your life where your needs are not being met? Get to the root cause of or triggers for your behavior.

Burnout Symptom 5:
Feeling Ungrounded or Out of Control

If you are an earth angel who gives a lot to your family, friends, or colleagues, your energy might be going outward so often that you have gotten out of the habit of coming back in to ground yourself. Coming back to center is coming home. When we are grounded, we feel safe, confident, and calm. It's not something you will feel all the time every day, but if you can feel this way a majority of the time, it will very much help you in your mission as an earth angel. It will also help you avoid burnout.

Earth Angel Antidote

It's true that each individual might have different ways to help themselves feel grounded. I have a close friend who never misses her Friday night hot yoga class. If she's had a challenging week, it brings her back to center. Another friend thrives on community—being around people with a shared experience or goal grounds her. For me, I find self-care and doing my work in the world very grounding. Whether it's daily meditation, drawing an oracle card for an inspiring message each morning, feeling connected to Spirit during a walk in nature, spending time with loved ones, watching a favorite movie or listening to a favorite musical artist, cuddling with a pet, or making an appointment to speak with a counselor— or all of the above—find the magic recipe of ingredients that help keep you grounded. Then when you feel ungrounded or out of control, you have something to reach for and hold onto to steady yourself.

Burnout Symptom 6:
Feeling Bitter Instead of Optimistic

As much as we talk about the ability to feel more grateful and the power of hope, some people might just be naturally more pessimistic than others. This may not have as much to do with their environment or experience as their natural disposition. Some people have idyllic childhoods but are naturally more cautious and guarded and pessimistic, while someone who has faced intimidating challenges consistently throughout life is optimistic and open and more prone to saying yes than no. Pessimism gets a bad rap. There is such a thing as healthy pessimism, where we are more discerning about opportunities we are presented with and people who come into our lives. Folks who are naturally more pessimistic are probably naturally good at this healthy discernment. Earth angels tend to be sunny, bounce back quickly, and are always ready to give someone a second chance or the benefit of the doubt. While earth angels are good at seeing the best in people, those with a healthy natural pessimism are equally good at seeing the aspects of others that are toxic, sabotaging, or even dangerous. I once had a friend who was naturally pessimistic. At first I tried to talk my friend out of his pessimism, but as our friendship grew over the years and I spent more time around him, I realized that a lot of my friend's observations about people or situations in my life were actually on point and catching my blindside. His healthy pessimism balanced my natural optimism and gave me a fresh perspective that I desperately needed in some cases.

Realize that developing a healthy pessimism or having someone in your life who can give you a pessimistic take on things can be very valuable for an earth angel. Sometimes pessimism protects us. But with earth angel burnout, I'm not talking about a pessimism that protects, but one that holds you back. If you are an earth angel who finds yourself no longer connected to your natural optimism, always focusing on the negative in others or situations, or anticipating the worst, it could be a sign of burnout.

Earth Angel Antidote

The reason earth angels are naturally optimistic is because as helpers to others, we need to be able to uplift, inspire, and see the positive potential in every person and situation. If you are cut off from this natural optimism, you might feel cut off from yourself or not quite feel like yourself. When you have lost your natural optimism is a great time to connect with other earth angels and let their natural optimism reignite your own. Even simply reading a book that is incredibly positive can really bring you back into the fold of healthy optimism. Even TV shows have their own distinct energy. Brené Brown's 2019 Netflix special *The Call to Courage* has an energy that is so uplifting while also being very realistic about the challenging aspects of life. When people watch Brené speak, it's not just the truth of her words but also the energy behind them that actually changes the energy of the people in the audience.

Look around and find someone who inspires you. Inspiration is a great antidote to unhealthy pessimism. Hunt for articles online about people who experienced miracles, or ask your friends to share a story where grace helped them achieve something they thought was impossible or how the right people or opportunities showed up at just the right time for them. Feed your soul with optimism, and soon you will be naturally generating it on your own again. The great thing about healthy optimism is that it changes your perception of the world, and that changes your experience of the world.

Burnout Symptom 7:
Thinking No One Cares for You

This is a very interesting symptom of earth angel burnout—it might be largely true. While some symptoms are secondary, the thought that no one takes care of you might be a primary realization about people in your life. The problem is that you might have taught or trained them (consciously or unconsciously) that you don't need to be cared for. Having read up to this point, you already know that earth angels are natural givers who care deeply about the well-being of people in their lives. Earth angels have a tendency to think of others before themselves because earth angels feel good when they help others. By being so giving to others, you might have sent the message that you don't need anything back.

Earth Angel Antidote

Instead of blaming others, take stock and see if you have been sending the message that you don't need anything from the people in your life. Are you the type who soldiers on and suffers in silence? If you experienced childhood wounding where you were taught that asking for your needs to be met is pointless because they won't be met anyway, you may need to practice being vulnerable with people by letting them know you need or could appreciate help. Give others a chance to change the dynamic in your relationship by voicing your needs and desires. Start small; asking for small things gets you in the habit of asking for help. In time it will feel more natural to make a request, even when the ask is significant.

Burnout Symptom 8: Being Deeply Moved by Small Acts of Nurturing from Others

Have you ever had someone do something small for you, like a stranger hold the elevator, and the moment stays with you, giving you a warm feeling all day? Or maybe a niece or nephew or friend's child climbs in your lap and asks you what is wrong, comforts you, or tells you they love you and this small, tender act of kindness brings tears to your eyes. Sometimes our sensitivity is heightened, and the world just seems like a magical, wondrous place where every small event sticks out to us and we feel especially present in the moment.

Other times we might be deeply touched by acts of nurturing and attentive kindness from others because we feel starved of this energy, like how wonderful a nice meal fills us when we are really hungry. Our intense emotional reaction to this nurturing can let us know it's something we are craving and need more of. If we don't get enough of this energy—from ourselves, a pet, our loved ones, our clients, our health-care providers, or even strangers—it can lead to burnout in a big way. An Episcopalian priest once said to me that our souls need feeding daily, and part of a healthy soul diet is feeling nurtured.

Earth Angel Antidote

Get more nurturing into your daily life. As Byron Katie wisely observed, the best person to mother each of us is ourselves. Become someone you can go to and count on for nurturing, whether it's something small like going to the grocery store every week to make sure delicious and healthy food is waiting for you when you come home from work, or something bigger like ensuring you have a safe, comfortable, and inviting home or car.

You might also consider who in your life you can rely on for nurturing—maybe a massage therapist, Reiki healer, counselor, coach, or an intuitive. A heart-to-heart chat where the focus is on you with a kind, loving friend or cuddling with a family member or pet can be extremely nurturing. Perhaps it's not a person but a place that feels nurturing, like waking up in your grandmother's house or putting your toes in the grass or sand at your favorite nature spot. Making sure you feel nurtured is a great cure for earth angel burnout. And by learning how to nurture yourself, you will be better able to nurture the other people in your life in the unique way only an earth angel can.

Burnout Symptom 9:
Letting Your Self-Care Slip

I have been on the phone many times with earth angel clients and asked them how they were doing with their diet, supplements/medicine, sleep, and exercise routine and heard them say, "I know what I need to do and have all the stuff, but I have not been consistent lately." Letting your self-care slip can be either a symptom of burnout (you are too tired or overwhelmed to stay on top of it) or it can be a cause of burnout (without proper self-care, you become tired and overwhelmed), although it could also be a chicken-or-egg scenario. Letting self-care slide to a self-sabotaging level is something that can happen to anyone, not just earth angels. But since earth angels are often so concerned with the well-being of others (e.g., being "good" employees prone to over-giving), earth angels might be more prone to burnout.

Earth Angel Antidote

First, figure out why you let your self-care slip. Is it something obvious like life becoming suddenly busier? Maybe it was something that happened slowly over time, where you just gradually got out of the habit of taking care of yourself in small ways but now your entire self-care routine is just a distant memory. It could also involve something more subconscious, like not feeling worthy of good self-care. Determining the cause for your self-care sabbatical is just as important as taking action steps to take better care of your physical and emotional well-being.

Now practice some healthy self-care discipline. Make a list of ten things you could do more consistently to take better care of yourself. These should not be all daily things, and you don't have to aim for perfectionism, which could make you abandon your intention. These self-care goals could be as simple as getting more sleep, spending more time in nature, doing meal prep on Sundays so you have healthy lunches all week long, starting a side hustle to help you save money or pay down debt, restarting a daily meditation practice, telling someone how you really feel or what you really need, scheduling a monthly massage, attending a weekly yoga class, giving yourself a hug, making a date to catch up with a friend, taking a nap, or seeing your healthcare provider for a tune-up.

Burnout Symptom 10: Noticing a Significant Change in Your Outward Appearance

Are you someone who loves beauty and enjoys getting dressed for the day, whether heading off to school, the gym, or the office? (I'm the type who wears statement earrings to the grocery store.) Yet you might have gone through periods where you stopped even noticing how you dressed. In one of her books, author and life coach Cheryl Richardson mentions a time when she went to the store and found a hat that just called her name. When she got into her car and looked at her purchase laying on the passenger seat, she wondered why she was getting so excited and feeling such intense emotion over a hat. She began to cry as she slowly realized the hat symbolized a time in her life when she took great pleasure in fashion and putting together outfits. She had become so busy in her career that this part of herself had been pushed to the side and ignored until now. Maybe you have a certain ideal weight that you believe suits your frame, genetics, and health (a very different value for everyone) but lately you have either lost or put on a lot of weight. While we all change as we age, sometimes you might notice physical changes in yourself that are stress related, like nervous habits or tics that are normally not a part of your physical life. The change might be as simple or obvious as being so busy, or depressed, or burnt out that you haven't gotten your hair cut in a long time.

Earth Angel Antidote

Sometimes, how we look physically can reflect what is going on emotionally or mentally. What is going on inside you that has changed your appearance? Sometimes appearance changes are natural. When I get more lines on my face or more gray hairs at my temples, it might take me a few days to adjust. What throws me off is not seeing those statement earrings smiling back at me in the mirror; without them, I just don't feel like me. Sit with the notion that a physical change might be natural, like aging or intentionally changing your look. If the change feels like a symptom of burnout, don't concentrate so much on changing the outside as changing the inside. Why are you burned out, dear earth angel? How can you make life better for yourself? Remember, that's what you came here to do—make earthly life better.

Burnout Symptom 11:
Feeling Physically Exhausted

This is something I know a lot about; I suffered from a chronic condition for years that involved exhaustion off and on. Those of you who have read any of my other books know I went on a healing journey (or what at times felt more like an odyssey) that involved cleaning out my gut bacteria, healing my intestinal lining, flushing out heavy metals, replenishing my vitamin and mineral stores, overhauling my diet, changing the way I exercised, increasing my self-love, balancing my hormones, and repairing my adrenals and thyroid. It sounds like an earful, but I know many of you have faced big health struggles or know loved ones who have.

For me, this healing journey meant always discovering new pieces to the puzzle. I went for a routine checkup and learned my thyroid was low and I had a severe vitamin D deficiency. My get-up-and-go had got up and left, as we say here in the South. My physical exhaustion meant that something was not right with my body, something that might also be true for people who are experiencing chronic conditions that have a main symptom of exhaustion. It wasn't quite true that my exhaustion was *caused by* or was *a symptom of* burnout—there was definitely an underlying medical issue.

For you, exhaustion might include being underslept, overworked, worrying too much, or being drained by those around you. That type of exhaustion is a symptom of burnout. Exhaustion without an underlying medical issue can be a classic sign of burnout for anyone, not just earth angels. Your body is saying, "I can't do things this way anymore. We need to change something here, fast!"

Earth Angel Antidote

If you have determined that there is no medical reason, work on pinpointing what is causing the burnout exhaustion and how to bring your body into a better state of balance. If you are a worrywart, for example (I suspect sensitive people are more prone to this), then you might have to do some healing around this issue to improve it, which can take time and patience. Perhaps you realize your diet or exercise routine is causing burnout and exhaustion, so you'll have to be firm with yourself until the new habits you adopt feel like second nature. Or you may have to negotiate healthier situations with roommates or family members or employers. Whatever changes or work you have to do to feel more rested and full of energy will be totally worth it in the long (and short) run.

Burnout Symptom 12: Not Asking for Things

Asking for things is powerful. While you might hear the occasional *no*, many times the only way you open the door to a *yes* is by asking. Asking takes courage, vulnerability, and wisdom. Earth angels who have a strong desire to help others might have forgotten the importance of asking for things for themselves. If you've stopped asking for things at work, in your relationships, or even from your divine angels through a prayer, *ask yourself* why. Maybe at the office you learned that asking was pointless because your needs were not going to be met anyway. Perhaps you have a strong and independent warrior aspect to your soul and dislike the vulnerable feeling of asking. It's common for us to run on autopilot, so maybe you have just gotten used to not asking being your default mode. This is why it can be empowering to set aside regular time to check in with yourself and review and reflect on your life so you can evaluate your conscious and subconscious patterns.

The bottom line is that not asking for things leads to burnout because you aren't getting the extra help and resources you require. Sensitive earth angels might be especially prone to not asking, as they can pick up on the uncomfortable energy and emotions asking might produce in someone else.

Earth Angel Antidote

Practice asking for things from the people in your life. Start small if it feels more comfortable, like asking for a table that would be more to your liking when a host steers you to a table at a restaurant that doesn't suit you. If you have a big ask for a family member or colleague, for example, spend some time practicing how you will ask. Use creative visualization to imagine them having a positive or neutral reaction to your ask, even if they end up saying no. Remember that hearing no is not the end of the world, nor does it have any bearing on your worth or potential. In time, you will develop a thicker skin or healthy callus around the word no so that you won't have such an intense emotional reaction when you hear it. A no is not always personal; sometimes people would love to say yes but aren't able to. And sometimes a no is a blessing in disguise, or the universe protecting us from something that is not in our highest good. The universe often responds to our actions, so just the mere act of asking—no matter what answer you hear—is a sacred act and might open unexpected doors for you that you hadn't even knocked on.

Burnout Symptom 13:
Feeling Like Life Is Punishing

Life is meant to be a balance of challenging things and stuff that is easy and simply flows. Of course we will have times when the balance feels off. But if we lose our equilibrium for too long, or the way we are facing these challenges is unsustainable, life can begin to feel punishing. You might even ask yourself, "Was I born to suffer?" This is a question that, sadly, clients have asked me.

Perhaps the hardest part about feeling like life is punishing is that no one else knows exactly what we are going through, because everyone's life and challenges are unique. If you told me you were going through a very challenging time, I would have sympathy for you but never pretend to have all the answers, either. Yet when we feel like life is punishing and joyless, it can lead to burnout quite quickly. If you cannot shift any of the major puzzle pieces in your life, it might be about going for some simple pleasures; cut yourself a break where you can. It's no fun to feel like Cinderella, and I'm sure that if Cinderella were a real person she would be talking to her therapist or health-care provider about this intense burnout she's experiencing.

During very rough times you might persevere for others until things improve, like knowing how important you are to a child, friend, sibling, parent, pet, coworker, student, neighbor, etc. Sometimes it's easier to be strong when we have someone to do it for, as it can give our lives more meaning. When we can't connect daily with the meaning or the point, days feel like a punishment.

Earth Angel Antidote

There's an old saying that sometimes it's not what you are carrying but the way you are carrying it. Imagine if you were in college and had a lot of heavy books you carried in your arms instead of using a backpack. Sit with the idea that there might be a better way to carry some of the challenges you are currently facing. Ask your intuition and your divine angels for guidance. Ask loved ones, coworkers, and health-care providers for suggestions too. Make a list of simple pleasures or ways to cut yourself some slack that you could implement now. Take stock of your resources. Is there an abundance of anything? Like time, money, faith, or friendship? If so, use that to your advantage. Make sure you're not trying to prove anything to someone else or yourself that you can go it alone.

Even when we face extraordinary challenges and life asks extraordinary things of us, we are always expected to and indeed must rely on the help of others to complete our divine missions. None of us were meant to go it alone, and that includes earth angels. If life feels punishing, find ways to change the dynamic so you don't feel you are in it on your own, like sharing your struggles with a trusted friend or counselor. Make a list of meaningful things in your life. It might be as simple as knowing that your customers would miss your smile and banter if you were not there to hand them their coffee every morning, or that your grandma would be lost without your weekly call. Earth angels have a talent for finding great meaning in what others might consider small, everyday things. Find the little miracles happening all around you—especially the ones you create.

Burnout Symptom 14:
Feeling Cut Off from Magic, Grace, and Miracles

It can be especially depressing to be an earth angel who feels cut off from magic, grace, and miracles. That's because earth angels live and breathe magic, grace, and miracles. Those things feel as necessary as air, water, and food. The reason this feeling can lead to burnout is that it can actually become a self-fulfilling prophecy. If you feel disconnected from divine assistance, you will not be as apt to recognize it or utilize it when it arrives. You also won't be as apt to ask for it either.

Humans are powerful spiritual beings, just as powerful and dynamic as the divine angels we call on for assistance. Because we are powerful beings gifted with free will, heaven can help you even more when you reach out to ask for things. You will be helped regardless, even if you don't believe in Spirit or never connect consciously with your divine angels. Yet free will is like every human's magic superpower. Use it well. Spirit wants to keep you on track with your destiny and will do everything possible to make sure that happens. However, the universe is a very receptive energy, so the more you ask for things, or look for and expect help, the more grace, magic, and miracles you will experience.

Earth Angel Antidote

If you are an earth angel who feels cut off from grace, magic, and miracles, you may not have been making enough time for your spiritualty or honoring that side of you that believes in grace, magic, and miracles. The most obvious reason for this is feeling tired or overwhelmed in your life. See if you can make some space every day or once a week for your spirituality. It could be as small as mindfully connecting with something you are grateful for that day during your morning commute, or as big as signing up for a weekend workshop with one of your favorite spiritual teachers.

Look for small moments of grace in your life, like when a meeting is cancelled so you can have a long lunch with a friend. Read about huge miracles that happen in the news. Think about the miracles, big and small, that have occurred in your life in the past. Connect again with the energy of magic, grace, and miracles, and you will see evidence of it in your life and alleviate symptoms of earth angel burnout.

Burnout Symptom 15: Wishing Someone Would Come Along and Save You

Speaking of Cinderella, a character mentioned in the context of life feeling punishing, I think we all occasionally wish that someone, a Prince Charming, would come along and save us from our life circumstances. While heaven will offer help so that we may save ourselves, it's rare that someone steps in and lifts us out of all our chaos or worries.

If you keep having fantasies of someone saving you, or you look to other people to take sole responsibility for aspects of your life that only you can fix, it's a good sign you are feeling burned out. Instead of looking for the knight in shining armor to save the day, address the root of the problem: You're probably so burned out that you no longer feel capable of managing or navigating certain challenges. We all come up against times like this.

Earth Angel Antidote

It might be best to take a temporary break from tackling the problem head-on, worrying, and overthinking it. Instead, tend to your overwhelmed nervous system. Do things that are calming and soothing and increase your self-care routine of clean diet, good supplements/medicine, rest, exercise, finding greater meaning in your existence, and time with loved ones. Once you are feeling stronger in general, you will feel more capable about meeting this challenge and your intuition will come up with best next steps once you feel rested and centered.

Sometimes temporarily stepping back from an issue is the most proactive and productive thing you can do to help solve it. Step away for a bit to give yourself perspective; when you reengage with the issue later, you will look at it with fresh eyes from a fresh angle. Get out of the story you have been telling yourself so that you can try to write a new storyline.

Burnout Symptom 16: Letting Other People's Opinion of You Become Your Opinion of Yourself

When we aren't burned out, it can be much easier to take criticism from others. If you feel centered and grounded, you can take people's opinions about you with a grain of salt. It's easier to see if there is anything useful in the information and disregard the rest. Kind of like panning for gold, you can sift through the pebbles and dirt for what's worth keeping with some time and detached reflection. After all, sometimes people's opinions about others or the outside world have much more to do with themselves than anything else. You might have a supervisor who is disappointed in the way their career turned out and jealous of your talent, so they tell you there is no hope for you to advance—in this case the opinion is much more about the supervisor's issues than yours. Alternatively, you might have an old friend tell you something about yourself that rings true but really hurts, causing you to realize there is an issue you need to work on.

If you are experiencing burnout, a sharp word or cutting remark or critical observation from someone else can send you into a tailspin. When we are burned out we lose touch with ourselves, so we may no longer be able to discern, "Is what this person saying true? Or is part of it true and useful information?" If you have developed a codependent relationship with a boss, partner, or child, you might have gotten so used to tracking or trying to control or absorb their emotions that their opinions are no longer something you run through your own "truth detector" in your mind and heart, but rather take as face-value fact.

Earth Angel Antidote

If the opinions of other people about you are really unsettling, or you are having trouble discerning what in their opinion resonates or feels true for you, spend some time alone. This is a great way to center and reground yourself in your own energy. If your boss or a colleague is disappointed in your performance, take some walks alone in nature to ground yourself before deciding what your opinion is on the situation. Check in with your confidence, as well—is the tank a little low? If so, why? Did you do something that disappointed yourself, or did you just take someone else's opinion too much to heart?

The funny thing about opinions is they change all the time. One month your partner might be annoyed with you or nagging constantly, and the next month they act like you hung the sun and the moon. It's important for sensitive people and especially earth angels to maintain a strong emotional center or core. Because they can so easily tune in to the energy and emotions of others, earth angels have to watch not being so easily swayed by them. Spending nourishing time alone can help heal earth angel burnout.

Burnout Symptom 17: Finding Yourself Consistently in Relationships, Roles, or Situations That Are Not Win-Win

This can be difficult to admit to yourself—are you usually in situations or relationships where there is an equal amount of giving and receiving, or do you find yourself giving more than others and feeling drained? If you have a lot of drama in your life or you dread seeing certain people's names pop up on your phone or dread certain people popping into your office, the scales may not be balanced. Ideally most situations in your life should be a win-win, meaning everyone involved feels like it's a win for them. There will be times when this isn't true, but if you feel burned out, you might look for a pattern where there are more situations that are not a win for you but are serving the other people involved quite well. Pay attention to your feelings, which can be a great barometer for earth angel burnout.

Earth Angel Antidote

Set aside a week night or Saturday afternoon to take stock of the main relationships in your life: romantic partnership, close friendships, family bonds, and any other important relationships like business relationships. Get out a sheet of paper and write down for each relationship what is a win for you and what you believe is a win for the other person or people involved. Do these wins balance out? Then ask yourself how much you are giving and how much the other person is giving. Remember that it's not about things being perfectly balanced or perfectly balanced all the time. You might have a good friend who is going through a really rough patch, so naturally you are giving more right now in that relationship. Yet is there a relationship in your life where you are consistently giving 70 percent while the other person is giving closer to 30? Keep an open mind. You might find that you are the one winning big and another person is carrying more of the load.

Burnout Symptom 18:
Not Having Any Space in Your Life

Are you going from dawn 'til dusk? Is life one long to-do list? If this is an everyday experience for you, it will certainly lead to earth angel burnout. The soul needs some time to rest *and* play. Often I will tell a client that they would benefit from an hour of sanctuary time a day. It should ideally be low-stimulation time where the nervous system can relax and recover from any stressful events or just the hustle and bustle of the day; time where you feel free and that nothing is required of you. A client may think, "An hour a day? I *wish*." If it isn't an hour a day (e.g., you work full-time and have small children), shoot for thirty or even twenty minutes. If you have to play catch-up on the weekend, set aside more than an hour where you can unwind. In a scenario involving young children, unwind time might come in smaller quiet moments, such as snack or nap time. Earth angel parents may have to be quite cunning about finding some space in their schedule. At work, space might look like shutting the door to your office for half an hour, stepping outside, or turning off your computer for a fifteen-minute break to clear your energy. Creating space in your life can lead to breakthrough ideas and big, positive change.

Earth Angel Antidote

Train yourself to create more space in your life. Schedule more time in between clients. Linger over your lunch at an outdoor café. Arrive fifteen minutes early to an appointment and meditate until it begins. Say no to helping someone with a passion project that *you* aren't passionate about. Overscheduling ourselves is habitual, but it can also be unlearned. Look at your own schedule and see if anything can be taken off your plate.

Did you volunteer for something at your work or child's school that you really don't have time for? Practice saying no with love, like "I wish I could help with that right now, but I've got too much on at the moment." Are there chores you are doing at home that other people in the house could help out with, or should you consider hiring someone to clean the house or keep up with the yard? Make some room in your life and don't worry about how you will fill it. The space will help you unwind and unfurl your energetic earth angel wings so you can be more relaxed and present every day…and way less burned out.

Burnout Symptom 19: Suspecting That Everyone Else Has It "Easier" Than You

Cinderella seems to be a theme in this book, and this fictional heroine has many lessons to teach. Do you feel like you are scrubbing the floor in rags while the people around you (or your evil stepsisters) are laughing it up at the ball? Having regular, bitter thoughts that you have it harder than everyone else is a sign of earth angel burnout. While it's true that everyone's life experience is unique and some are born into lives of ease, comfort, and luxury, no human escapes this earthly experience without suffering, and I would go so far as to say significant suffering. Even a person with what we'd consider an easy life could and will still experience loss and pain. It may not be the kind of suffering on the same level of those born into difficult circumstances of poverty and a lack of safety experience, but it's still suffering. And all suffering, to the person who is feeling it, is significant.

Recently I ran into an old acquaintance who is a professor, and we began talking about how it can be challenging to get steady work or tenure at universities. My acquaintance was running through names of colleagues and what colleges they were currently attached to throughout the country. These other professors sounded like they were doing well and thriving. My acquaintance was up for tenure at his institution but felt nervous about it; his pinched frown and downward gaze showed how frustrated he was. Then his energy shifted, his expression transformed into one of lightness, and he said, "But I can catch myself now when thinking that no one has it as hard as me," he confided. "It's a mind trap I used to fall into, but I realize it's not at all true. And that helps a lot."

When you find yourself always comparing your life to others and feeling like you got the raw end of the deal, it's time to turn your attention back onto yourself. Stop comparing and sending your energy outward for a moment and focus on your life and how you can feel more blessed in it.

Earth Angel Antidote

Start a gratitude practice and focus on what you are grateful for that is very unique to your life. Maybe you were given a chance in your career that colleagues and friends envy. Perhaps your finances are a mess but you and your partner have a love, commitment, and bond your friends would love to experience. Maybe you often tell people, "I've always been healthy, knock on wood," with a sense that this is remarkable and a blessing you can't quite understand but are grateful for.

The next time you are comparing yourself to someone else, check in to see if this comparison is healthy. If jealousy lets you know there is something that someone else has—free time, the money to travel, a loving partner—that you want, it might be healthy to try to bring some of what that person has into your life. Maybe you can't take the three-week trip to eastern Europe your aunt went on, but perhaps there is a day trip close to home or a weekend getaway that would scratch the itch and make you feel blessed instead of like Cinderella.

Burnout Symptom 20:
Being in Several Relationships Where
You Don't Feel Valued, Honored, or Seen

Do you ever feel like you are simply playing a role to someone? Are you just "the breadwinner" or "the nurturer" or "an employee," and the people you play this role to don't see or value you as a whole person? Being seen, valued, and understood is so important to our well-being. Feeling invisible at work or home or in a friend group can have negative effects on our self-worth, confidence, and even self-love.

Maybe you would be really great at a different job in your company, but when you apply for a promotion, your manager tells you that you are wasting your time. Yet you know in your heart what your talents are, and that you have great potential, which this manager refuses to acknowledge. Perhaps you are gay or bisexual or pansexual, and while certain loved ones know this about you, it is a taboo subject in the family that is never discussed. If we don't feel like we are loved fully for our authentic selves, it can eat away at a relationship and create an unhealthy dynamic. This does not mean you have to leave the job where the manager won't acknowledge your potential or leave the family that will not acknowledge your sexuality. But what you are able to achieve at that job, and how much you give to it, should be considered. And the level of intimacy and trust you are able to build with certain family members could be lower. Discern if not being seen and fully appreciated by people in your life is a rare or isolated occurrence or a pattern that needs shifting.

Earth Angel Antidote

When others do not see and honor us for who we really are, we can forget who we really are. If you are in several situations and relationships where you don't feel seen and honored, write down a list of who you really are. You might write down roles like "mother" or "brother," but you can also write down archetypes, e.g., "performer," "comedian," "earth angel," "warrior," and so on. Then make a list of people in your life who really see you and honor you for your authentic self. These could be close friends, family members, or work colleagues. Invest more time in these relationships, and you will be investing more in living your authentic life. Spending some reflective time alone or doing your favorite activities can get you back in touch with your whole self.

Burnout Symptom 21:
Empathy Paralysis

A client described the idea of empathy paralysis to me as "…like when you are even afraid to walk out of the house because you might step on a bug." Another way to describe it is when you are so concerned about other people's feelings that you become immobilized. Empathy is something all humans and especially earth angels experience not as a punishment but as part of their internal GPS system. Like the cameras or sensors on a car that alert the driver that they are about to collide with something while in reverse, empathy can also go into overdrive. Those sensors can become so sensitive that they can make us afraid to drive anywhere.

Remember that empathy was never meant to isolate you—by contrast, it was meant to help you better navigate being out in the world. Feeling empathy paralysis, where you are overly concerned about hurting other people, could mean you need to adjust your sensors or just take a break from stimulation for a bit and nourish your overwhelmed system.

Earth Angel Antidote

Turn your focus inward instead of worrying about the rest of the world. What has your sensors overstimulated? Are you physically or mentally run-down? Has your self-care routine fallen by the wayside? It might be that you have not been taking the best care of yourself lately and your sensors are malfunctioning. Or perhaps you are worrying about everyone else as a form of projection to avoid dealing with something that happened to you. Did something traumatic happen that you have been avoiding sitting with, like an upsetting conversation at home or work? Have you suffered a major disappointment recently? Did a loved one let you down? Did you let yourself down? Maybe you actually did hurt someone's feelings badly, and now you have a bit of PTSD around this issue. Sit with some of these questions over the next few days and take yourself in for a tune-up so you can hit the road again feeling more like yourself.

Burnout Symptom 22:
Taking Things Too Personally

This concept has already been covered and is something that an earth angel's sensitivity will naturally set them up for more than other people who are not as sensitive. As a sensitive child, you may have heard things like, "You take things too personally." Please note that I'm not talking about feeling things deeply, wanting to remain tender instead of too tough, or demanding respect.

Have you ever interacted with someone who was distracted or in a bad mood and immediately racked your brain to see what you did to cause it? You may not have seen or interacted with this person for days or weeks, so you mentally review your previous interactions with them for clues. Then you find out from a mutual friend that the person has been stressed at work or is having fights with their partner. Suddenly you feel so foolish torturing yourself when their negative mood had nothing to do with you. As an earth angel, you might even wish you had spent your worry time trying to cheer this person up instead.

A different way this might manifest is having a strong reaction to an innocent comment that was not directed at you. Or you might often misconstrue people's motivations, thinking a leading question was meant to set you up when really the person asking is looking for a way to help. Overreacting to playful teasing can fall in this category.

Earth Angel Antidote

Hit the pause button before immediately reacting to other people's comments to give yourself a chance to let the comment land. Use your feelers or engage witnessing energy to decide what this comment means and the most appropriate reaction to have. Taking things too personally can mean we feel overly defensive. In what ways are you feeling attacked right now in your life, and by whom?

If you are continually feeling like the comments or teases of one person are over the line, it is not a symptom of burnout but rather a warning from your own system that your boundaries are being crossed in an unhealthy way. In that case, take some kind of action where you address the issue with this person, bearing in mind they may have honorable intentions and not be at all aware they are upsetting you. Taking things too personally can also be a sign of a sensitive person's nervous system being frazzled, which is the most common cause of earth angel burnout.

Burnout Symptom 23:
Numbing Out

If sensitive people do not get enough retreat and recovery time, avoid looking at an unhealthy situation in their life, or put off making a healthy change, they can numb out with food, alcohol, drugs, shopping, excessive exercise, or binge-watching. Over time, numbing out in one of these ways can become a coping skill that the sensitive person uses to navigate the world. Sometimes the sensitive person could take something, like binge-watching or shopping, that might be fine in moderation and use it as a shield to block out the world and their own sensitivity.

Earth Angel Antidote

If numbing out by overdoing something to an unhealthy level has become a self-care routine, just substitute something else to help you retreat and recover that is healthier, like reading an informative nonfiction book or walking in nature. If you suspect you have a real addiction, it may not be as easy to substitute healthier activities. That's okay. Everyone has an addict inside, and your sensitivity and this activity may have triggered yours. Get help from professionals or recovery groups and tools. Be gentle with yourself. Having an active, self-sabotaging addiction does not make you a bad, weak, or unworthy person. It does make you an earth angel who needs and deserves help.

A Few Last Thoughts on Earth Angel Burnout

My goal wasn't to make you overly concerned about burnout; instead, I was inspired to make it a central theme because I so often meet earth angel clients who are dealing with some degree of burnout. Though often it's minor, recognizing a few of the twenty-three symptoms I've listed here can help earth angels be aware of the burnout sooner rather than later in order to take action.

Occasionally I come across a client who is so far into earth angel burnout that when I talk about the character traits of earth angels, they say something like, "I used to be that way, always wanting to help and caring about others. Then life got so hard that I lost touch with all that." If almost all of the earth angel burnout symptoms we outlined in this chapter feel true for you right now, it's natural that you won't currently resonate with the idea of giving to others. As someone who has experienced extreme earth angel burnout myself, I can happily report that a full recovery—and then some—is entirely possible. Don't be afraid to reach out to health-care professionals for help: go to your doctor for a checkup or see a counselor on a regular basis. Get help from friends, family members, and coworkers. Make small changes in your life to heal your burnout; consider bigger changes, although small changes can work miracles.

If you're looking for one surefire method to deal with burnout that will offer relief to anyone, anywhere, at any time, whether their burnout is minor or full-blown, it's significantly upping your self-care game, which we will cover in the next chapter.

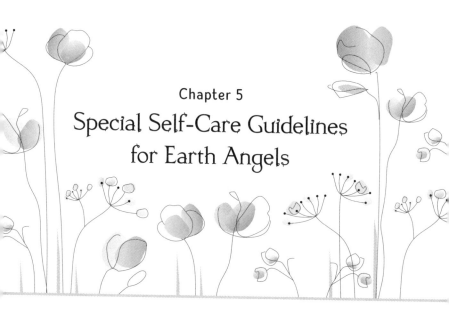

Chapter 5
Special Self-Care Guidelines for Earth Angels

Self-care is important to the physical and emotional health of all humans, earth angel or not. So please feel free to adopt for yourself or suggest to others any of the techniques outlined in this chapter. When I look back at my life, there are times when I was very on my earth angel game, and other times when I felt very disconnected from that energy. The difference was self-care and balance. When my life was in balance and I was able to practice great self-care, I was so much more hopeful, open, and giving. Sometimes how in balance things like our health or finances are may not totally be within our control. Hopefully the information in this chapter helps you control what you can. The more effort an earth angel puts into fine-tuning a self-care routine and being aware of its significance, the more able they will be to help others and fulfill their earth angel mission. As well, the amount of time spent on self-care or attention paid to this aspect of your life will fluctuate throughout your life.

I hope some of these core principles are ones you can come back to throughout your earthly journey; this might be a good chapter to keep in mind when you are feeling stressed or run-down. In those moments, play a game with your intuition by opening this book to a "random" page and seeing what message you receive. While this chapter is specifically about self-care, all the sections of this book are designed to help support earth angels taking good care of themselves. I would love to see you get more proactive about self-care and up your self-care game.

Self-Love as a Tool for Transforming Your Life

Humans can be very hard on themselves, and earth angels are no exception. Earth angels can have a high bar set for themselves regarding helping others and being compassionate, as these qualities are so crucial to an earth angel's purpose. An earth angel might feel bad for days about snapping at someone, while another person who is not an earth angel might be able to shake off the same incident or put it into perspective rather quickly. While it might be natural for people who are more sensitive to ruminate longer on these types of experiences, it's vital to know when to let go of such an experience and move on. There should be a strong foundation of self-love that helps us recover, and recover more quickly, from any setback or poor choice we experience in life.

Self-love is the key to unlocking not only more peace or happiness in our lives but also the key to unlocking more potential and achievement in our lives. When we are being punishing or unloving toward ourselves, our energy shrinks or withdraws, while the energy of self-love is motivating and expansive. If you can love yourself through some of your biggest regrets or challenges, you are not only supporting yourself emotionally, you are also activating a powerful alchemical component to change and miracles. Self-love is a key to unlocking more of the good stuff in any area of your life.

I have been told time and time again by divine angels that when we judge ourselves or blame ourselves in our thoughts for something in the past, it keeps us trapped in that same energy that created the situation we dislike so much. If you are in debt due to a shopping addiction, for example, it might have started as a way to numb yourself as a sensitive person. Perhaps you look back and realize that you have spent thousands of dollars on clothes you really didn't need or even enjoy over the past year. Now you are kicking yourself for not spending that money more wisely, such as paying down bills or loans. Or you might be stressed about money now and wish you had used some of that clothing fund to create a savings cushion for yourself.

Learn the lesson, hold yourself accountable, and feel all the feelings. But do not abandon yourself by being cruel or harsh with yourself in your thoughts or actions. You might have to admit you have a problem and talk to someone about the underlying issues that caused it. It could take time, patience, and work to shift your pattern. But if you can meet yourself with love and compassion, you will move forward and create a new reality for yourself much quicker. As an earth angel, imagine how you would feel if a friend came to you with a similar problem. While you might be saddened by their addiction, your first reaction would be to comfort and reassure them. Your challenge is to meet yourself with the same nurturing and healing energy you give to others.

If self-love is an issue for you, please don't get trapped in a cycle of being mad at yourself because you aren't good at self-love.

Again, we want to nip that punitive energy in the bud. Sometimes when we have a harsh attitude toward ourselves, we act in self-sabotaging ways.

Self-love has a magical ability to shift your life dramatically and open doors that have remained shut to you. I don't totally understand and cannot fully explain how it works, but I have come to accept self-love as a metaphysically transformative fact of earthly life. Trust this fact, and allow self-love to work for you in miraculous ways. Love is a powerful, healing energy.

The Influence of Childhood on Self-Love

You might also want to examine if there are deeper issues for you around self-love, such as not getting as much nurturing or love as you needed during childhood. In even the best of circumstances, being a parent is very challenging, and indeed many people act as parents under challenging circumstances. Looking at childhood wounds isn't something you do to punish or judge your parents, but simply something you do to better understand how you might have absorbed or mirrored, as a sensitive child, the way your parents treated you. These patterns can be carried into adulthood subconsciously and hold us back from enjoying our lives more fully.

If your parents were very busy and did not pay you much attention, for example, you might have learned to be invisible. The invisible child archetype is something Caroline Myss talks about in her work, and it might have been a coping skill adapted in childhood to deal with a situation where you did not receive much attention. You might have also been the abandoned child, if, say, your parents died or became absent in your life.

Did you have a parent who was very hard on themselves and judgmental? Usually the way people treat others is a reflection of how they treat themselves, so if you had a very stern and unforgiving parent, they were probably that way to themselves in their own mind. This might have become a way of relating to yourself that felt normal and therefore comfortable. Examining childhood patterns and wounds can be very enlightening as far as understanding why you may not be showing yourself enough love.

I think parents today are much better about letting kids know how special they are. Part of loving yourself is feeling special and recognizing your unique strengths. While my parents were very busy and sometimes absent, I luckily had teachers and other family members as well as my parents who pointed out many of my strengths. As we age, I think close friends can be wonderful at pointing out our talents and gifts.

What were/are your parents or guardians like, not just as parents but as people? What were/are their hopes and dreams? You might have grown up with a parent who had a bad drug or alcohol addiction or severe mental health issues. Or you might have grown up in a fairly "normal" house that still created a complex family dynamic.

For many clients, I've found that childhood can set the tone for how they treat themselves as adults. Please don't feel that if you had a very dysfunctional childhood, you've been set up for a lifelong unhealthy relationship with self-love. Sometimes a challenging childhood can be an invitation to even more self-love, because you as an adult can look back at the child who deserved better and give yourself the best experience you can as an adult.

Earth angel adults naturally make our own patterns and traditions and develop new ways of loving and supporting ourselves, yet sometimes parts of the outdated and unhealthy family programming can still be operating in the background. When we are trying to up our self-love game so that we can up-level our lives, it can be useful to examine some of the old family programming and lovingly update the software.

Earth Angel Exercise
Identifying Childhood
Patterns around Self-Love

As a reminder, this exercise is *not* about blaming or shaming your parents. As well, it could bring up some strong feelings such as anger or sadness, which is normal. Remember that the more you let yourself feel something, the sooner you can process it and receive its message. It's only when we really sit with our feelings that they'll pass quicker and leave us feeling much lighter afterward. If any of the questions that follow bring up memories or feelings that are overwhelming or too difficult to sit with alone, please pull back for a time or speak with a loved one or counselor.

Hopefully you will find this exercise enlightening, as it will allow you to map and track your self-love habits and patterns. Simply sit with each question and see what comes up for you—it might be a feeling, a memory, or an a-ha! breakthrough realization. If you were raised by people other than your parents (e.g., grandparents, foster parents, older siblings, and so on), please use your experiences with them to answer these questions. Have a journal handy in case you want to jot down some of your reactions:

1. How did your parents show or tell you they loved you growing up?

2. How has the way your parents expressed their affection for you influenced the way you express affection toward yourself? Sit quietly until you receive an answer.

3. Were your parents good about self-care? What, if any, were some of their self-care routines?

4. Have you adopted any of your parents' healthy self-care routines? Sit quietly until you receive an answer.

5. Did your parents or guardians or the folks who raised you make you feel unique or special in a positive way?

6. Did your parents' opinions of you somehow negatively or positively affect your opinion of yourself? Sit quietly until you receive an answer.

7. Did your parents ever tell you what your strengths were and did they share what they felt your weaknesses or areas for growth were?

8. Do you reflect and make time to celebrate your strengths and work on your weaknesses or areas for growth?

9. Was love conditional in your household? Like based on good behavior or good grades?

10. How can you be conditional with yourself regarding self-love? How do you show yourself unconditional love?

11. Did your parents ever push you toward something that did not resonate or feel natural to you, like pushing you to participate in a sport or pushing you to get a certain major in college or pushing you into the family business?

12. Have you ever pushed yourself to achieve something as an adult when it did not feel authentic, or found yourself going after a goal only to please others?

13. Did your parents seem to have life mapped out for you as a child, saying things like, "When you become a doctor" or "When you become a mom" or "When you go to this trade school"? Or did they not seem to offer much guidance or direction at all?

14. How have you mirrored this at times as an adult, either not paying enough attention to where you are headed or not being flexible enough about the journey?

15. Did your parents seem happy and fulfilled, or was it mirrored to you as a child that these things were not important or unrealistic?

16. Whether you were told outright or it was something you picked up on subconsciously as a child, were you ever made to feel by your parents that having you was a blessing?

17. Were your parents run-down or overworked?

18. Have you developed a pattern around being run-down or overworked, and if so which parent or guardian modeled this for you?

19. Did your parents believe in healthy touch, like snuggling on the couch with you or kissing you goodnight before bed or hugging you in the morning before dropping you off at school?

20. How do you get healthy touch today? Examples might be from a pet, a romantic partner, hugs from a friend, or healing touch from a massage therapist.

21. Were you left alone a lot as a child? Did this teach you to enjoy your own company and develop creative hobbies?

22. Did your parents stress the importance of well-being? Taking good care of yourself emotionally, physically, and financially? What areas were they best at?

23. Are there bad habits—like smoking, eating junk food, codependent relationships, or excessive debt—you "picked up" from your parents? How have you healed this?

24. Did you feel your parents loved you and did the best they could, but needed better tools? What type of tools?

25. Did one of your parents struggle with perfectionism?

26. Do you believe your parents blamed you for something in their lives they did not like or did not turn out as planned?

27. Did your parents sacrifice a lot for the family, or did they have a balanced, fulfilling life outside the family?

28. Did your parents place importance on joy and savoring life?

29. Do you think you adopted any positive or self-nourishing beliefs about joy or savoring life from your parents?

30. Do you believe either of your parents were earth angels? If so, how well did they deal with burnout?

31. Can you identify any family members or people like teachers and babysitters who had a significant positive influence on you as a child who were also earth angels?

32. Were any other people in your family sensitive? If so, how did they utilize and manage their sensitivity?

Make a list of childhood patterns you do not want to repeat, and then turn them into positive mantras like:

- "I make nurturing myself a priority."

- "Seeking out support during challenging times is my default mode."

- "I recognize and celebrate what is amazing and unique about me!"

- "I insist that people I love speak to me in a respectful manner and I offer them the same respect."

Earth Angel Exercise
Feeling into Self-Care/Self-Love Action Steps

Sometimes actions speak louder than words. There is a lot of emphasis on changing thoughts in modern self-help, which I believe is so powerful. Yet changing our actions can be even more powerful. Use your feelers—that sensitive part of you that is like invisible antenna and can feel into an idea or situation or person for intuitive information—to decide if these self-care/self-love action steps feel warm, lukewarm, or cold for you right now.

Deciding if something metaphorically feels warm or cold for you is a way to see how interested your intuition is in pursuing something or how important something might be right now. If a self-care/self-love action step feels warm it resonates strongly with your intuition, and you might feel excited or very intrigued with this self-care/self-love action step and want to try it out right away (or it might resonate strongly because you know it's something you need to do but have been putting off). If something feels lukewarm, it's a self-care/self-love action step to think about but nothing to rush about. You might feel curious about this self-care/self-love action step or have mixed intuitive emotions. When something feels cold, it means it's not attractive or intriguing at all. The feeling could be your intuition saying, "There's not much here for you with this action step, or at least not much in the near future."

Please note that feeling into things and sensing they are cold is different from resistance. When a friend suggests something, for example, you might feel a strong and immediate resistance. You could even use language that expresses an absolute, e.g., "That would never work for me." Then years later you take your friend's advice, it works wonders, and you wish you had tried this much sooner. As I've gotten older, I've become quite curious about things I initially resist very strongly; often in the past those things were actually things I needed to be open to. Feeling something cold has a calm energy, where resistance to something helpful often has an intense or emotional energy.

Jot down in pencil how each self-love action step feels to you—warm, lukewarm, or cold—after reading it. Then go back and pick two or three of the steps that felt warm and start on those right away. This exercise of seeing if something feels warm, lukewarm, or cold is a great intuitive test you can perform on anything. However, it's never a substitute for using logic or consulting an expert.

1. Buy yourself some comfy new socks or slippers.

2. Tidy up your office, files, or desk.

3. Start a weekly or monthly savings plan.

4. Get a side hustle to pay off debt more quickly.

5. Sleep in on the weekend.

6. Buy yourself flowers.

7. Make a list of your greatest accomplishments and the lessons you learned from your biggest challenges.

8. Write a love letter to your body describing everything you think is beautiful about it and several reasons you are thankful for it.

9. Stop procrastinating on something you know will make you feel relieved and happy to have taken care of.

10. Ask for help with something that has you so stuck you cannot move forward on your own.

11. Treat yourself to a massage, energy attunement, or appointment with an intuitive.

12. Give yourself an oracle card reading or pick one inspirational oracle card for yourself every morning for a week.

13. Take a long soak with your favorite bath salts and listen to a great podcast.

14. Make yourself your favorite meal.

15. Tell yourself a hard truth you don't want to look at.

16. Tell someone else who has been consistently hurting your feelings that you need something in your dynamic to change.

17. Forgive yourself for a grudge you have been holding against yourself. Ask a divine angel or anyone else like a counselor for help if you need it.

18. Take your most persistent and negative self-talk thought and turn it into a loving and supportive mantra.

19. Go to the grocery store and buy the ingredients to eat clean and healthy for two weeks.

20. Take a long walk in nature, attend a gentle yoga class, or perform some other soothing exercise.

21. Allow yourself to put off something that can be put off easily and safely.

22. Share with someone you love how proud you are of yourself regarding a recent accomplishment.

23. Ask for something small from someone.

24. Ask for something big from someone.

25. Mark off a sacred day or afternoon for yourself on your calendar so you can play, relax, or do something that interests you.

26. Do a swap with a parent you know and trust where you each take the other one's kids for the afternoon so you can get caught up on things at work or home or just take a nap.

27. Do yourself a favor—whatever that looks like. What's the first thing that comes to mind?

28. Make a doctor's appointment or checkup you know you need but have been putting off or have felt too busy for.

29. Call an old friend for a heart-to-heart and make sure you have plenty of room to talk about yourself instead of just listening and offering advice.

30. Spend time in person with a loved one you know will be fully present with you.

31. Take yourself out to lunch alone with a great book or magazine for company.

32. Take the supplements and medicine you know you need every day, not just when you happen to think about it.

33. Do something for yourself that you know is the right thing to do. What's the first thing that comes to mind?

34. Attend a concert, art opening, sports game, or other big event that makes you feel more alive.

Saying No with Love

Is saying no hard for you? If you are an earth angel, even mildly refusing people you love or who are hurting or are in need can be very tough. Yet saying no to others can sometimes be a way to say yes to yourself—a great act of self-care. Personally, it can be hard for me to say no to my husband; sometimes it can hurt your heart a little to say it. So here are some things to bear in mind that can help you with the process when you have to say no.

Usually, saying no to someone will not kill them. There can be exceptions to this, such as if they are asking you for a major organ. I do know people who have donated organs to loved ones and even strangers, and it's always an amazing act of courage and mercy. Outside of these extreme situations, most people will be able to live through or survive your refusal. The reason you think your no might seriously damage this person is probably because as someone who is sensitive, you can really feel some of the intense need or desperation or longing the other person is experiencing. Or maybe you can feel the relief they are expecting to feel when they expect you to say yes. Sensitive people can be prone to anticipatory stress, so they are anticipating all the conflicting and challenging emotions their no will produce in another person—hours, days, or even weeks beforehand.

If you are sensitive and have to lovingly say no to someone, this is another ideal time to practice mindfully tuning in and out of people. Retract your feelers and engage witnessing energy. Parents of small children do this all the time. Have you ever seen a parent say no to their kid in a store when the child really wants a toy or piece of candy? The parent stays firm and often unemotional while the kid goes crazy—begging, yelling, crying, rolling around on the ground. I don't recommend always appearing unemotional when you say no to someone you love—and hopefully the other person won't start rolling around on the ground in protest!—but the takeaway here is that these parents have learned to tune out of their child's emotional reaction. To some degree, you might need to do the same to get better at saying no.

The hardest times to say no can be the most powerful and lead to the biggest transformation. But when you feel strongly about something, whether you end up compromising or the other person comes around to your side of things, it's important to honor yourself and stand your ground. This is a huge part of self-care, especially when we are talking about things that are central to our well-being.

How many times can you look back at the decisions your partner or parents or children or friends or colleagues pushed you into that you felt were not in your best interest? Maybe some of these things you said yes to (when you wanted to say no) even blew up in your face or had long-lasting and unpleasant consequences. We've all done it many times, so don't beat yourself up. And while you might feel some anger toward others at these memories, remember it takes two to tango. Since earth angels can have a strong desire to make others happy, they might be prone to making others happy by saying yes to things they shouldn't.

Because earth angels' collective mission is to help others, they can mistake that mission for people pleasing. If you truly want to help others, the way to do so most effectively is to say a healthy no. You might save them from a poor choice, teach them a hard lesson, or help them find their bottom, or make them more self-reliant. In these instances, saying no is a short-term hit on a long-term investment.

Practice saying no, and practice tuning out of someone as you do it. You don't have to tune all the way out, as parents pretend to ignore children during a tantrum, but if someone is in need and you really want to help but can't, it might not help to tune in to their pain and suffering at that moment. Think of the information you get from your feelers like water going through a hose; "adjust" the tap so less water or empathic information comes through. Be an objective observer. Or you could picture consciously retracting your feelers (which are beautiful, colorful, and strong) or invisible antenna. You might even picture yourself putting protective socks or clothing around your antenna. The time to use your feelers in this scenario might be after the person asks but before you answer. You could politely request some time to think the matter over, then retreat and feel into the situation from a safe distance.

At its core, tuning in and out of people is about focus. For example, after you say no, if you keep thinking about the request you turned down and imagine how disappointed they were with your no, change the channel in your mind. Think of something else entirely. Or think of all you've already done for them emotionally and materially, which is a way to reframe. You could even pray for them quickly.

Part of the reason you don't want to totally tune out another person's emotions is that this is one method you use to determine what is going on with them and connect into your own intuition for guidance. So perhaps you use your feelers more sparingly and engage a higher percentage of witnessing energy—it doesn't have to be an either/or scenario. Because earth angels like to do things with love, it's most comfortable to say no to people we care about in an authentically loving way, something that requires some open emotional exchange where we are also emotionally present.

Here are some tips for saying no with love:

1. **Practice saying no ahead of time.** Do a dress rehearsal of saying no in your mind or even out loud with a friend. This is especially helpful if the person who wants your yes is coming to you with a big ask, like a raise, or when your no will be a big deal to them. Your refusal might set a precedent, like giving your teens a stricter curfew, something that will add to the emotional weight and drama of a situation. Practicing your refusal gives you the opportunity to discern how to phrase it with loving language, and it prepares you for some of the likely fallout or kickback you'll encounter. Remember that although forethought and planning ahead can be helpful, if you do too much of this it can actually cause more anticipatory stress instead of less. You want to feel prepared going into saying no, but you don't want to overthink it to the point that it becomes bigger in your mind than it needs to be.

2. **Ask for space so you can make sure your no is firm.** Whether it's a big ask like letting a family member move in with you or a smaller ask like watching someone's pet for the weekend, asking for space to think it over before responding gives you time to feel strong and grounded about your no. This asking for a reasonable amount of time to think it over before answering also gives an earth angel time to step back and separate their own feelings from the feelings of the person asking. While earth angels might be tempted to say "maybe" or give someone temporary hope to spare their feelings, it can actually have the opposite effect

and make things worse in the long run. Saying no with love doesn't work as well if you are wishy-washy. Sending mixed signals or giving someone false hope can create extra drama and hurt feelings.

3. **Offer clear reasons for why you felt the need to say no.** Give the other person a look into the reasoning behind your no. If they are pitching a project to you and you had to decline, it could be a teachable moment for the other person to improve their next pitch. Or it might help them understand that your no had nothing to do with the quality of their presentation—their style just was not the right fit for you. Offering someone knowledge or a lesson is an act of love, as it also lets the other person know that the no wasn't just a quick or hasty refusal, which can feel unloving. You had real reasoning behind your decison.

4. **Assure people that your no is not a reflection of the way you feel about them.** You might love your child more than anything in the world but lack the financial resources to pay for their college education or wedding. Sometimes we would say yes in a heartbeat if we could, but we have to put our own needs first. Conversely, you may not particularly like a colleague but have given their ask true consideration. You might diplomatically let them know that while you have had differences in the past, it had nothing to do with your decline, which was based on more practical concerns. You might add, "I was and still am looking forward to getting to know you better and working closely on something; [what you've proposed] just isn't the right project for me right now."

5. **Remind yourself that saying no can be a great act of love or moment of grace for someone else.** Although it has negative connotations, the word no isn't always a bad thing. A closed door from one person or opportunity can be what opens another door that could be better or more authentic. For example, you might have to tell someone that you don't want to be with them romantically. While you are not the ideal person for the asker to marry, your no helps them eventually find a soul mate. If someone in your life is an addict, or needs to find a bottom with a certain self-sabotaging pattern, a no from an earth angel like you could build resilience in this person or point them in a new, healthier direction. This is what some might call tough love.

6. **Find a way to say yes to someone in another way.** Part of your no might be offering other ways you can be of assistance. Maybe you cannot loan them your car tonight, but you are happy to drop them off and pick them up from their shift. Maybe you aren't sure what you could say yes to, so you let this person know you're open to other ideas about how to be of assistance. It might require some brainstorming. Earth angels very much want to be of assistance, so this technique still lets you show love by helping, just in some other way.

Realistic Optimism and Staying Peaceful in Tough Situations

While some may naturally lean more toward optimism and others toward pessimism, earth angels are usually natural optimists unless they are experiencing severe burnout. We discussed previously the power of pessimism, and how a naturally more distrusting or pessimistic friend can be an important ally for the earth angel and help catch an earth angel's blind spot—especially where it regards always seeing the good in people and always wanting to give them another chance.

Some earth angels might be so naturally optimistic that it's hard for them to look at the other side of the coin, so to speak, or acknowledge that things are actually kind of rough in their lives at the moment. Because earth angels can be so concerned with other people's emotions, they can be the type that solider on and wear a brave face to the world—something that is especially true if the earth angel in question has a strong warrior aspect to their soul or if the earth angel faced many exceptionally challenging situations early in life that made enduring difficult or harsh circumstances necessary survival measures.

Part of an earth angel's self-care is allowing themselves to let their guard down and lean on someone when things are rough. Depending on others is crucial when an earth angel doesn't see life as magical and full of possibility, but it is also useful even in temporary rough patches or when things seem a little pointless. A great friend or therapist an earth angel can vent to is a valuable aspect of self-care. The first and sometimes hardest step for an earth angel is simply admitting that things are particularly tough or challenging in their life at the moment.

Earth angels can tend to take on the role of rock or cheerleader in their relationships, which means they always carry the torch of encouragement and faith. That torch can get quite heavy if there are no moments to set it down, take a rest and, most importantly, let someone else carry it for a bit. We all need a moment to put the pom-poms aside and acknowledge the challenging emotions and situations we're experiencing. Even when some spiritual value or lesson can be found in a situation, it still might really be awful—and that's okay to admit.

While pessimism has a valuable place in the world (indeed, earth angels need to be able to be real when things are tough-going), an earth angel's fuel is optimism. To believe the world can be a better place, to believe people and situations can heal, to believe there can be even more miracles and magic on this planet—these are the reasons earth angels came here. They wanted to be part of helping to make all that good stuff a reality on earth.

Having a grand, expansive optimism is important—after all, there were people who believed humans could fly through the air hundreds of years ago when no one yet saw evidence of it, and these visionaries turned out to be right. Yet during especially challenging times, earth angels might find realistic optimism more helpful. Since earth angels love to inspire people and give them hope, if the earth angel believes this hope realistically, it is like putting a higher grade of fuel in their tank. This is not different from the power of positive thinking; it is simply the power of *realistic* positive thinking. The realism in this sense refers to what we have evidence of that we can probably accomplish in the present or in the near future. We need to see evidence and progress to keep hope alive and help it grow.

A perfect example of realistic optimism is Paul McCartney's Meat Free Monday campaign. While Sir Paul is a vegetarian who does not consume meat as a lifestyle choice, he understands that for many people, simply giving up meat one day a week is a big ask. Paul's campaign got many people to think more mindfully about their meat consumption and how it was affecting not just animals but the planet. If this former Beatle had set out trying to get everyone to stop eating meat altogether, he may not have gotten very far. But by being realistically optimistic, his program got people's attention and made a big impact. Little actions add up to big change.

To be clear, being realistically optimistic still leaves room for miracles. That's important, because miraculous things happen all the time—and earth angels *love* a good miracle because it reminds us that life is magical. Small or huge, it makes no difference.

As it relates to self-care, what small action step can you, as an earth angel, take that is realistic *and* will make you feel more optimistic about a challenging situation in your life or the world? What is the first situation that comes to mind? It can be related to personal things like finances or health, or it can be related to larger things you are part of, such as your community's overall health or even helping the planet at large.

Earth Angel Exercise
Filling Up Your Optimism Tank

Have you been struggling with something so big or been watching something so devastating play out in the world that you have lost touch with hope and optimism all together? Here are ways earth angels can get their optimism on when they've lost touch with hope:

1. **Spend time in nature.** Since nature is so grounding, taking a short walk or long picnic in nature might make you feel more like yourself. As an earth angel, you are naturally optimistic, and it's easier to tap into that natural optimism when you are grounded. If you have an outdoor space, make it cozy and inviting and spend more regular time there, like eat breakfast outside or grab your laptop and catch up on emails outside. Nature is grounding because as someone who is sensitive, you

automatically tune in to the energy of the trees, plants, rocks, water, and sky around you. If you don't have an outdoor space, get to a local park or greenbelt, or start a windowsill garden or treat yourself to fresh flowers.

2. **Read something inspiring.** Sometimes a positive book can remind earth angels that while really bad things happen in life, really good things happen too. Find an article online or a book at your local bookstore that has a super positive, uplifting energy. The book might be in the mind, body, and spirit section, or it could be an inspiring memoir or a laugh-out-loud humor book. Use your feelers to find the right choice.

3. **Call someone for a pep talk.** Earth angels are great at pep talks. While a pep talk is just words, we have to remember how powerful words are—both what we hear others say and what we tell ourselves in our thoughts. Instead of trying to pep talk yourself, call someone else to get a jump start on your battery. Pick someone who knows you well, believes in you, and is usually encouraging. You can even text them first and just say, "Hey, I could really use a pep talk." It is powerful for an earth angel to ask for what they need; it helps them take better care of themselves so they can be a more powerful force for good in the world.

4. **Let yourself get angry or have a good cry.** When earth angels feel depressed or very pessimistic it could be a sign they are bottling up even stronger challenging emotions. Let yourself get angry by writing it all down in your journal or venting to a safe friend. If you've been holding back tears, let yourself have a nice cry—have tissues and whatever else you need ready. Letting out these negative emotions can

be very cleansing, and you might be surprised by how calm or refreshed you feel a few hours later. Then the pendulum of your emotions will naturally start to swing back toward hope and optimism. If you are in a major funk and crying or venting does not provide any relief, don't be shy about reaching out to a loved one or health-care professional.

5. **Clean up your act.** Have you been eating well, resting, and taking your supplements/medications? When our physical body gets thrown off-kilter, it can have a big effect on our emotions. You can always get your health-care provider to test your vitamin and mineral levels as well as your hormone levels and thyroid function. Research or talk to your doctor about adrenal fatigue to see if that might be an issue for you.

6. **Use your sixth sense.** What does your intuition say about you becoming more optimistic? Does your sixth sense or intuition have a recommendation? Pick a number from one through six. Go with the first number that comes to mind. For me, that was hearing the number four and seeing the number "4" in my mind. So I'll go back to the fourth item in this section, which is about letting yourself express challenging emotions, and employ that whenever I need to get my optimism tank refilled in the near future.

Earth Angel Exercise
Spoiling Yourself

Earth angels are such givers that they need to nourish themselves by regularly giving back to themselves. Ideally this happens in small ways every day. If you're super busy at work, or super busy taking care of an elderly relative or small child, it might be helpful to carve out a few hours once a week where you can really give back to *you* and spoil yourself. Sometimes being selfish is a very healthy thing.

We've all had that feeling when we are spoiling ourselves, maybe buying something beautiful for the house or playing hooky from our to-do list or allowing ourselves to get lost in a creative project, when it just feels so good and right to be selfish. Use your feelers to see when being selfish, and putting yourself first, is the best option. Being selfish in a healthy way can make you feel intense delight or relief. Although that's not all it might make you feel. You might have to block out someone else's emotional reaction to your selfishly healthy move, or you might have to get used to spoiling yourself without feeling guilty.

Step 1
Grab a journal and something to write with.

Step 2
Make a list of all the ways you love to spoil yourself. Remember that being selfish in a healthy way might initially trigger some pangs of doubt but should give way to a feeling of lightness. If you are not used to spoiling yourself, just be patient as you practice this self-care art and create a new healthy habit. You might also think of some things that seem harmless, like overeating or overdrinking, but the more you ponder the way it makes you feel afterward, you realize these are not the best ways to spoil yourself. That's good stuff to get clear on too.

Step 3
What stops you from spoiling yourself? Once you write down your list of ways you love to treat yourself right, you might be left

thinking, "Why don't I do this more often?" Answer your own question here. Maybe real-life responsibilities to others simply keep you from spoiling yourself as much as you would like. Or maybe you have feelings of guilt when you spoil yourself. Where is this guilt coming from? Your childhood or cultural programming? Does someone else make you feel guilty or are you doing it to yourself?

Step 4
Check in with this list you created of ways to spoil yourself once a week to see if there are any you can indulge in. It's very fun to find new ways to spoil yourself and keep things fresh, so keep adding to this list. Remember, too, that spoiling yourself does not have to involve spending much—or any—money.

Step 5
As you get used to spoiling yourself more often or become clear on what being healthy in a selfish way looks and feels like (allow yourself the grace to make mistakes as you figure out what self-ishly healthy looks like for you), take mental note of any positive changes in your attitude or mood. Does spoiling yourself make you happier, more relaxed, more confident, more assertive?

Make Life Feel Sacred
Many earth angels feel a deep connection to Spirit, whatever that looks like for them individually. You might think of Spirit as God, the Goddess, many gods, Source energy, the Universe, love, or something you can't even quite name yet feel deeply. Earth angels need to feel that life is sacred and that even when they are

experiencing challenges or great suffering, Spirit is with them and has a plan … or is coming up with one on the fly.

Earth angels are often the type of people whose faith is only increased by challenging times. They can be the folks running around encouraging everyone else after a natural disaster or act of war, holding a space of light in unthinkably dark circumstances. Earth angels can shine in these moments, because part of their mission here on earth is to uplift and assist others and even act as emissaries of Spirit. Earth angels can be an example of faith in action or carry Spirit's message of faith to others with their words. This might explain why some earth angels feel such a deep connection to Spirit that they devote their lives to spiritual pursuits, becoming priests, meditation teachers, or spiritual healers.

In my intuitive sessions with clients, occasionally past lives will come up. If the idea of past lives does not resonate with you or match your spiritual beliefs, you could think of past lives as soul archetypes. If someone believes they were a monk in a past life, you might consider that their soul is strong in the monk archetype—the kind of person who would enjoy living in a closed spiritual community of prayer, study, artistic pursuits, volunteer or charity work, and meditation. Often people who are earth angels will show up to me as having a past life where they took holy orders of some kind. They might have been a nun or monk, or they might have been the wise woman or man of their village. This is because in this lifetime and others, deep in their soul, they have always felt a strong connection to Spirit.

I was raised by an agnostic mother who never spoke about Spirit or took us to any kind of organized religious service growing up. Yet when I was in middle school I erected a little altar where I would kneel, cross myself, and pray. In high school I discovered Wicca and bought a deck of tarot cards. The study of

Kabbalah and Buddhism and many other spiritual traditions was something that always drew me in during my late twenties and early thirties, even though I came from a family where there was no spirituality. In my mid- and late thirties, I attended an Episcopal church. Something in my soul yearned for spirituality and sought it out again and again. It was how I reminded myself that life was sacred. Feeling a connection to Spirit and that my existence was sacred was a self-care technique that saw me through the rough times and enhanced the good times.

If you identify as an earth angel, find ways to make your life feel more sacred, more connected to Spirit. Some might do this out of a sense of obligation to their religious beliefs or because it seems like the right thing to do. For earth angels, acknowledging the Divine and making life feel sacred is a powerful act of self-care.

Earth Angel Exercise
Making Life Sacred

Below are some tips for making life feel more sacred and connecting to the Divine.

1. **Listen to sacred music.** Is there an artist or a genre of music that feels sacred to you? It might be meditation or Reiki music, with gentle melodies layered over each other. It could be an artist whose work has spiritual themes like Enya, Loreena McKennitt, Kirk Franklin, Prince, or Deva Premal & Miten. Perhaps you love gospel music, folk, or traditional Celtic or Indian music. Whatever makes you feel more alive yet also sends your mind and nervous system into a deep sense of peace is your sacred music. Put it on in the kitchen as you make dinner, in the shower as you

clear your energy with a nice scrub, or anytime you want to relax and feel more connected.

2. **Find a divination tool to work with.** I have a friend who likes to connect with the I Ching, the ancient Chinese divination text, every morning to get a message for the day. Sometime in the morning, usually before noon, I stop my workday and draw a single inspirational oracle card for myself to help me set the tone for the day. You might like to meditate for fifteen minutes at the end of the day or when you walk in the door from work and get a message from Spirit that way. Divination tools are simply ways to get more guidance from Spirit. While I believe strongly in using your own intuition to communicate directly with the universe, these divination tools are also powerful methods. And because you are doing something very mindfully—setting aside time to draw a card, consult the I Ching, or meditate—these practices can be a wonderful reminder of your connection to the Divine. Tarot, pendulums, runes—there are many tools that help us to interpret the Divine. When any of these divination tools work for you, it can remind you that the universe is a genuinely magical, sacred place. This sense is something earth angels have always felt to be true and love to find evidence of.

3. **Do something where time stops and you forget your earthly life.** You've probably heard people talk about getting lost in a healthy escape activity where they lose all track of time. It's almost as if they enter a place where time and space don't have the same meaning and they aren't even aware who they are. Creative pursuits can make people feel this way; free of their earthly worries, they are in the zone,

as some say, a spot out of place and time where they feel their soul connection more strongly. Find an activity that makes you forget all your earthly cares and be fully present in the moment. Life feels much more sacred when these activities are a regular part of our lives.

4. **Look at people and situations in your life from both an earthly and spiritual perspective.** Changing your perspective takes consistency, and you might be out of the habit, though if you are reading this book you are already familiar with the concept of looking at things from a spiritual perspective. You might look at an issue with your boss from an earthly perspective (which we might also call a practical perspective, although spiritual perspectives are just as practical) *and* a spiritual perspective.

The situation: Your coworker is never around and going through a lot in their personal life, yet they expect you to be the good soldier and take up the slack.

The earthly perspective: Your coworker really is going through a lot, and since you need this job and maybe even really like the position, it's important that you do what needs to be done to stay in their good graces. After all, they have most of the earthly power in this situation since they have more seniority. Yet from an earthly perspective, you only have so much time and energy, and you are concerned you're on the road to earth angel burnout.

The spiritual perspective: If you are an earth angel, you might initially sympathize with your coworker and want to work extra hard to make up the difference for any absences at the office. Yet over time you realize that this person always has some drama in their life (like most of us), and while they do need special consideration they also use this as an excuse to abdicate their responsibility. This could be a case where you as an earth angel have been put in this situation partially to learn the spiritual perspective to stand up for yourself. This might look like pushing back on your coworker when they try to make you stay late or do twice the amount of work you were hired for. You might start to feel like Cinderella, and while your coworker is not really an evil stepmother, just a struggling, ordinary person, the power balance and fairness is so off that you must take some action.

The resolution: In an earthly sense, this might look like asking for more flexible hours, a promotion, a raise—or all three. Perhaps it looks like having a frank conversation with your coworker or their manager. You might get advice from a friend in a similar situation or read articles online about this scenario by experts. It could even mean looking for a new job. From a spiritual perspective, once you realize that while this situation has been uncomfortable and very upsetting, you have learned a lot from interacting with this person, your coworker, in such an intimate way. While you need to have stronger boundaries with this person, you might also soften toward them when you see your coworker from a spiritual perspective, as some sort of sage who has entered your life to teach you something profound—getting better at taking care of yourself, standing your ground, not letting others take advantage of you, not playing the victim or letting someone else assume that role, or any other lessons. In this way, we can sometimes see difficult situations or relationships as an act of grace (*if* indeed it is an act of grace). When something has deep spiritual meaning for us, it's much easier to navigate and put into perspective.

5. **Treat your body as sacred.** I had a session with a client recently who had started doing a lot of yoga and had completely cleaned up her diet. She was treating her body much more mindfully, which was changing her energy. I could tell that this was going to positively affect other things in her life, namely her career and relationships. If life feels really *not* sacred right now, I get it. I've been there. We all have. Daily life might feel like one long, pointless or joyless grind. Something to be endured rather than savored. When we feel this way, it can also mean we feel we don't have much control over our lives. If you feel powerless to change your life and make it feel more sacred, start with your body and treating it as a sacred temple for your soul. Please, start there and other things will probably begin to shift, like your mood and energy levels and even things that seem to have nothing to do with your body, like how you feel about your job or your romantic life. How do you need to start treating your body as sacred? Firstly, what comes to mind when I say that? Do you immediately think of your weight, cleaning up your diet, developing a supplement regimen, starting a gentle exercise routine, giving up something like caffeine or sugar or alcohol, making peace with your body, or something else? Find ways to honor your body and treat it as sacred—it can shift your whole life.

6. **Keep visual reminders of Spirit nearby.** Since your relationship to Spirit as an earth angel is unique, what reminds you of Spirit will also be unique. If you feel close to Spirit

in nature or the energy of the earth best embodies Spirit for you, having fragrant herbs or grasses around the house can remind you that life is sacred. You could build a nature altar out of leaves, stones, twigs, berries, pine cones, and other items found in your immediate vicinity arranged into a tableau that feels beautiful or symbolic. If crystals remind you of Spirit, or a religious symbol like the Celtic cross reminds you of Spirit, display them where you can see them often or in a special spot in your home, like an altar area. Whenever I sit down to write, which I do most days, I set up a mini-altar next to my computer wherever I'm working that day. It consists of two large crystals, a candle, a small Reiki angel figurine, and the oracle card I have pulled for myself that day for inspiration. Another item I like to keep around are fresh flowers. Though not always in my budget each week to buy flowers, when it is, I enjoy keeping them where I can see them often. When I write they sit behind my computer and when I give a session to a client they sit in the windowsill of my office. Flowers feel special and sacred to many, which is why they are such a popular gift. Any earth angel friend will thank you for the gift of a modest bouquet...as long as they are not allergic to that particular plant.

7. **Create a sacred day or time of day once a week.** My husband and I both work for ourselves and are both passionate about what we do...so we can tend to forget to take time off. If you are an entrepreneur, you know that it's often long and irregular hours. We decided to try setting aside one day a week where we hoped not to be doing any work, just enjoying ourselves for some part of the day. This became

quickly known as sacred Saturday. My husband wasn't always able to take the day off because of certain projects, and I wasn't always able to take the whole day off. When he could not honor sacred Saturday, or I could only honor sacred Saturday afternoon, one of my favorite things to do was go to a café in our neighborhood, order my favorite meal, and spend a few hours drinking decaf lattes and reading a great book. You might have Sunday as a sacred day in your family, or you might have Monday evening, after a full day of getting back in the swing, marked off as a sacred time. I once had a friend who had a rule that nothing productive was done on Monday evening. He maintained that it was difficult enough getting into gear all day after the weekend, and Monday evening easy-style was a gentler reentry. Make your sacred day, morning, afternoon, or evening reflect activities that make you feel grateful to be alive. Gratitude is a wonderful way to connect with Spirit and feel the sacredness in daily life.

Earth Angels—Sensitive Psyches, Sensitive Bodies

An earth angel's sensitive nervous and energetic systems can sometimes translate to a more sensitive physical body, so if you have been identifying with the earth angel archetype, it's worth considering whether your sensitivity extends to your physical body. This isn't always the case, although in my experience working with clients, I have found this to be true for many.

Eating a clean diet and taking whatever supplements and medications work for you is just smart advice for anyone, earth angel or no. If you are thinking of making major changes to your diet or curious about what supplements you should try, it's best to work with a health-care professional, like a functional medicine doctor or a naturopath or anyone qualified whom you trust. Every earth angel will have a unique body with slightly unique needs. Certainly each earth angel will have their own physical histories as well.

Avoiding caffeine, alcohol, and sugar might be a wise decision as an earth angel, or at least consuming these substances more mindfully. An earth angel might feel the effects of these substances more strongly than other folks. Since earth angels have such a sensitive system that is easily overstimulated, just one cup of strong coffee in the morning might have some earth angels still buzzed and overstimulated into the evening. For others, it's about knowing your limits—how much caffeine, alcohol, and sugar you can consume without throwing your body off.

You might have also built up a tolerance to alcohol, caffeine, or sugar and be consuming more than is good for you—whether you are physically sensitive or not. Sometimes these substances can dull sensitivity and intuition so that when people give them up or begin using them in moderation, they experience a significant jump in their sensitivity and/or intuition.

Since sensitive people pick up more easily on subtle stimuli, a strong smell or loud noise might bother the sensitive earth angel more than the other people around them. You might have a friend who loves to go to a noisy and packed bar or café, while for you the experience is just simply overstimulating to your senses. This sensitivity in the body might even extend to feeling extremes in temperature more, or perhaps just having it bother you more. Earth angels might be the types who like to be prepared and fully bundle up in cold weather and need to know where the nearest fan or AC unit is in hot weather. While some people love weather extremes, earth angels whose sensitivity extends to their body may not find it as pleasurable to bask in the sun on a very hot day or hit the slopes on a frigid winter afternoon.

If you are an earth angel and feel as though your psychic sensitivity extends to your physical body, drink lots of clean, filtered water and eat organic when you can. You might be more easily affected by toxins and chemicals in your environment. A friend may like using chemical perfumes and bleach cleaner, though these same substances may bother you. While you don't have to treat yourself as precious, you should take extra care to live and eat clean. Many times this is also better for the environment, so you can feel good in your earth angel mission, knowing you are protecting the planet as well as yourself.

Earth angels might want to make sure that they are on top of any physical challenges that are an issue for them, whether that is diabetes, hormone imbalance, adrenal fatigue, gut health issues, having your fight or flight response turned on, etc. Make sure you are getting all the supplements you need and taking them in a form that is gentle yet effective. Having a healthcare provider who resonates with you can be a great ally in figuring out what your body requires.

Because earth angels are such feelers, they might feel comfortable working with healthcare providers with whom they feel a connection. Just remember that sometimes brilliant doctors can have a cold bedside manner. Make sure you are getting what you need; if the right doctor doesn't offer emotional support or feel warm and cozy, don't be afraid to seek that component elsewhere.

Since earth angels are very clairsentient, they might often experience physical effects when they receive intuition information. When a client and I are on the phone together during a reading and we hit on something very important, my intuition will give me this information by sending chills all over my body.

This happens usually a few times in every session. Sometimes the client will say, "I just got chills too!"

Earth Angels Take Care of Their Earthly Needs

While I don't believe in sacrificing joy or purpose just to create what feels like more safety in the material world, the older I get, the more I realize how taking care of our earthly needs—creating stability with our finances and homes—is a huge part of our well-being. When folks used to talk about healthy lifestyle, they rarely included finances, but wellness authors and experts today include financial health as a major part of well-being.

Financial health doesn't necessarily or solely refer to having lots of money in the bank, although neither should financial success be a source of shame. Many spiritually minded clients have expressed concern over making too much money, but I don't think there is any reason for money and spirituality to be separate. Having money means you can give to charities you love, support loved ones, or feel calmer and more relaxed so you can concentrate on your work in the world. It can also allow you the freedom to make choices that feel more authentic.

Many Americans live paycheck to paycheck; if that is your reality right now, I want to firstly thank you for purchasing this book. Sometimes even a twenty-dollar investment in yourself can be a big splurge. I have definitely had periods in my life when I lived paycheck to paycheck. Sometimes those were difficult seasons, and sometimes not having as much money increased my gratitude, brought me closer to loved ones or Spirit, and taught me the value of simple pleasures. Living paycheck to paycheck may be something you can work on improving or shifting, or it might just be part of the reality you have to surrender to right now. Whether you are independently wealthy or just scraping by, remember your financial status has nothing to do with your worth or how much your divine angels love you.

There can be great spiritual lessons in money issues. For me, having debt taught me to be more responsible, that there are consequences for my actions, that I have to find a way to pay my way in this world, that money doesn't have to control my happiness or peace of mind, and that accepting the monetary system is important in this earthly life. I once attended a spiritual author's talk where she described going through a period where she lost all her money and her home and had to start over from scratch. She said the experience taught her that material things were not as important as she thought. Winning the lottery might lead one to learn about the power of money and giving to charity; coming into a large inheritance and blowing through some of that windfall could teach us that our money habits aren't so great.

Years ago, I started making a significantly bigger income. I was finally saving, but not nearly as much as I should have been. Where was all the money going? After living paycheck to paycheck for so long, I was not used to budgeting or putting anything aside. Following that first year of increased income, my husband and my accountant confronted me: "Where did all the money go, Tanya? You should have a lot more saved." It was a tough lesson but one I had to learn. And then, just as important, I had to forgive myself for my mismanagement of money and move on from that experience to create a new money story. Childhood can play a part too. My mom never had a lot of extra money growing up, and we lived simply. Perhaps somewhere down deep I was more comfortable not having money, even though consciously I desperately wanted to improve my situation.

If the idea of past lives resonates with you, know that they can affect your money attitudes in this life. Perhaps you were very poor in a past life and developed a lot of fear around money and resources like scarcity issues. Or you might have taken holy orders in a past life that included a vow of poverty. Try to see money as a neutral energy. Keep working with your own energy around it by telling yourself that money is safe, and you have nothing to fear from it.

For spiritual people—and certainly earth angels—it's hard to sit with the idea that some people in the world have so much more than they could ever need while others starve. And it *should* be hard to sit with. As we are living on a planet where that is the reality right now, we have to find a way to work within this dynamic while trying to change or improve it. Money in and of itself is a neutral energy—it's not good or bad (we just covered this, but it's worth repeating). Perhaps what we do with money can reflect better or worse choices, but that is not the fault of money.

As you sit with some of the other information in this book, sit with the idea of being more mindful about things like your home, car, and finances. Earth angels might love to think about divine angels and Spirit and other magical, deeply philosophical topics, but it's just as important that earth angels make sure they are secure as much as possible. As an earth angel, you might not have been born independently wealthy as part of your destiny so that you are forced to go out and be of service to others to take care of yourself financially. Or you might be an earth angel who was born to great wealth as part of your destiny, and you use that money to start a free school for poor children or to support the arts in your community.

Your finances will probably ebb and flow over time, and you will have seasons when you have more or less control over your money situation. So work with where you are today. Forgive yourself for any money mistakes or mismanagement in the past, and take the lessons to heart as an act of self-love and self-care. Make sure you aren't just trying to be the earth angel who always worries about your spouse or your kids or the world regarding resources. Make sure you are also actively trying to resource yourself. My personal balance is giving to charity and trying to be generous with loved ones while still trying to take care of myself financially as only I can.

Earth Angel Exercise
Examining Money Attitudes

The following are questions for reflection about money. There are no right or wrong answers. I'm only trying to help you get clear on your current attitudes toward money. If something helpful or profound comes up for you, I'm very glad. This list of prompts could be helpful to go through whenever you are concerned about money, or if your financial status changes in a positive way.

1. Do you think it's important for you to feel financially resourced? Why or why not is this important for you?

2. Have there been times in your life when you have not let a lack of financial resources stop you from pursuing your dreams, feeling peaceful, or feeling joyful?

3. What are some of your biggest money regrets?

4. What are some of your biggest money victories or proudest money moments?

5. Who do you think growing up (father, aunt, brother, teacher, friend, fictional character, historical figure) most influenced you regarding your attitudes toward money? Think of people who influenced you in positive and negative ways.

6. What were some of your first memories of earning money for yourself? (This might have been getting paid for chores, babysitting, or a first job.)

7. How do you feel powerful about your financial situation today?

8. How do you feel powerless about your financial situation?

9. Have you been getting consistent intuitive guidance about a change you need to make regarding your finances?

10. Who do you go to for advice or support regarding your finances?

11. Do you have a financial role model?

12. Who are the financial professionals you interact with (bank tellers, mortgage brokers, financial planners, CPAs)?

13. Have you ever asked a friend or colleague who is good with money for their top five money tips?

14. What are some of the challenging emotions money brings up for you? Are you afraid of money or angry at money? Does thinking about money just make you feel depressed or hopeless?

15. How would you like to feel about money? Hopeful, empowered, confident, curious, excited, or safe?

16. What are some dreams or goals you have for yourself financially?

17. Do you have anyone to talk to about your money concerns, like a partner or friend or therapist? Or is there a famous money author or guru you follow?

18. What one small action could you take today that would positively affect your finances?

19. What big action step could you work toward over time that would positively affect your finances?

20. Is there any area of your life where you could save more money?

21. Could you make improving your finances a game or a goal that gives your life more purpose? How else might you make the process more enjoyable or meaningful?

22. How could you stop judging or blaming yourself regarding your money?

23. Do you have any addictions regarding money? This could be a shopping addiction or being addicted to financially bailing out someone in your life regarding money or an online gambling addiction.

24. Do you feel independent in your money situation or dependent on someone else?

25. Do you catch yourself negatively judging people for their financial situation, whether they are homeless or a billionaire?

26. If you could ask divine angels to help you in some way right now with your financial situation, what would you ask them for?

I hope these prompts have given you some clues to any subconscious blocks or negative patterns you have about money and also inspired you to make any positive money changes you're able to employ right now. If you cannot do much to positively change your financial situation for the moment, getting clearer on your money patterns, attitudes, and goals will help you make more mindful money choices regarding your finances in the future.

Earth Angel Exercise
Forgiving Yourself with Archangel Michael

You might be wondering why I chose Archangel Michael for this exercise. It struck me that forgiving yourself for something in the past—whether it was a money mistake, a relationship issue, or sabotaging your self-care—can take a lot of courage, something that Archangel Michael specializes in. Other archangels you might work with for this exercise instead of or in addition to Archangel Michael include Archangel Chamuel (who can offer gentle, peaceful energy), Archangel Raphael (who can bring healing to any area of your life), Archangel Metatron (who specializes in life reviews), Archangel Gabriel (who is closely connected to sensitive men), or Archangel Ariel (who helps women realize they are stronger than they know).

Any and all archangels you choose to work with will be sitting with you, lending their energy and expertise during this exercise. If you are sensitive to energy, you might feel an energy shift after you call an archangel in with your thoughts or a quick prayer. Archangels are available to help as many people as need them. Once you request help, the archangel will be with you very shortly. As well, some archangels might already have been assisting you throughout your life without ever having been called upon by you.

Step 1. Get clear on what you want to forgive yourself for.

Pick the first thing that comes to mind. If several things come to mind, chose the one that you think would probably be easiest to forgive yourself for. You can go back and do this exercise later for any issues, even the very difficult and painful ones. However it might be nice to start with something you think you could make quick progress on to get you excited about the concept of forgiving yourself regularly.

Step 2. Sit with the idea of what it would feel like to forgive yourself.

You already know what it feels like to hold a grudge against yourself on this one—it might be energetically heavy, shaming, or defeating. Imagine what it would feel like to accept this happened, forgive yourself, and move on. Does your energy automatically feel lighter and more optimistic? Make note of any energy changes that occur, even if they seem minor.

Step 3. Fake it 'til you make it.

Start telling yourself you've forgiven yourself for this issue in your thoughts. Take a deep, cleansing breath in and out after you do, which will teach your body and nervous system to relax around this issue. If your mind challenges you on this forgiveness, tell yourself you have learned your lessons from the experience. You can even write the lessons down in your journal. You might also tell yourself that you'd like to make it right by moving forward to do better in the future but just can't accomplish that if you are always looking backward, judging and shaming yourself for the past, and keeping yourself trapped and immobile in that energy. Keep faking it till you make it with forgiveness.

Step 4. Imagine walking away.

Imagine this situation you want to forgive yourself for as an object, like a rock. See yourself putting the heavy rock down and walking away. You might lay it down on the dusty earth or a rough patch of brown, dead grass. Where are you walking to now? Picture your favorite nature scene—a field of wildflowers, a snowcapped mountain peak, a sandy beach. Feel the sun on your face or the wind in your hair. Create whatever details are nurturing, expansive, and pleasing. This is where you are headed by forgiving yourself. Sit here as long as you want in this place, with your archangel companion(s) by your side. You might imagine sitting down cross-legged, while your winged friend sits down next to you. What words of wisdom or comfort or encouragement does your archangel communicate to you? Maybe they simply reach out and hold your hand, fill you with warm and healing energy, or give you the strong sense that all is well.

———

I hope you enjoyed this chapter on self-care. I believe that self-care is the cornerstone of an earth angel's life. The cornerstone is the first and most important stone that is laid down in a structure. Every other stone exists in relation to the foundational cornerstone. In the same way, everything else we have already and will later discuss in this book—your sensitivity, your relationships, and your destiny—is greatly affected by your practice of self-care.

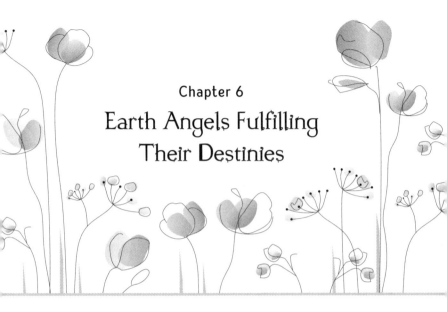

Chapter 6
Earth Angels Fulfilling Their Destinies

I f you're an earth angel who is anything like me, you want to know why you are here. You're always looking for the deeper meaning in events or pondering spiritual questions. Earth angels are the kind of folks who like to feel on purpose and that their life has some sort of intense spiritual meaning. So naturally earth angels want to feel that they are living in line with their individual destiny and connecting with Spirit about the bigger reason why we are all here.

I have some good news—you are definitely here for a reason. We'll discuss some of those specific reasons in this chapter. You have both a personal destiny, and you are part of the collective earth angel destiny. As an earth angel, your collective destiny is to promote healing, growth, and compassion. Your personal destiny is unique and will not play out or look exactly like anyone else's destiny.

Your Soul DNA

We've been steeping ourselves in the earth angel archetype, but I just wanted to touch upon the fact that this is far from the only soul archetype out there—or the only soul archetype currently operating in you. Some archetypes, like survivor or lover, you might call upon or employ as you need in life. Perhaps others—like warrior, rebel, or mother—you might come to feel are dominant soul archetypes in your own soul DNA. This means they are strong soul influences you came to this life pre-programmed with.

So you might be an earth angel with a side of philosopher, while your friend might be an earth angel who has a stronger leader archetype to her soul. Keep in mind we all have many different dominant soul archetypes operating at once, so you can certainly be a philosopher and a leader. Some soul archetypes are naturally part of us and may have started presenting themselves when we were a child. You might have enjoyed playing teacher as a child and forcing your friends to sit in your classroom, or you might have been a natural artist, spending hours in front of your easel drawing and painting. Perhaps these were how the dominant teacher and artist archetypes showed up in you even way back then.

Even if the earth angel archetype was not a major part of your soul DNA when you came into this life (and remember, it could have remained dormant until circumstances activated it), the earth angel archetype is one that any person can cultivate, just like any person can cultivate the diplomat archetype, whether it comes naturally to them or not. If you are curious about what other dominant soul archetypes you possess besides the earth angel archetype, look at what you most enjoy doing and also the roles life keeps forcing or guiding you into over and over.

Earth Angels: One Mission, Many Ways to Live It

You may have heard the saying that there are many paths to God. There are also many paths to an earth angel living out their destiny. Every earth angel's life will look different. So if you are feeling a bit at sea about what you "should do" with your life and now identify with being an earth angel, unfortunately there is no magic list of professions, roles, or locations that are ideal for earth angels. Because earth angels enjoy giving and helping others, you might think roles such as parent/guardian, nurse, healer, and teacher best suit the earth angel.

But you have to remember that each earth angel is unique, with a unique set of life circumstances and talents, unique soul DNA, and a unique personal destiny. None of our souls came here without a plan or some marching orders, and if the idea resonates with you then many have even been on earth before in past incarnations. While our destiny is fluid and always evolving, the person who came here to be a physicist at NASA probably is not the same person who came here to be a stay-at-home mom raising a house full of special needs foster children. This is why it's important to listen to your own inclinations regarding how you cocreate your life. Especially in the areas you have real control over.

That said, there are some things that all earth angels have in common regarding their destiny—they have a desire and talent for helping others. If you are an earth angel, you might find a coworker at your office or a regular customer at your store saying, "It's always just so nice to talk to you. Somehow you always brighten my mood and make me feel better." People might be drawn to earth angels for their optimism and warmth—at least when earth angels are feeling optimistic and warm. We can get as cranky and cold as anyone else when we are burnt out, out of sorts, or having a bad day.

If being of service to others, really feeling like you have helped others, and sometimes just creating a beautiful energy of compassion and nonjudgment wherever you go is the earth angel's true destiny, you can do this in any job or role. Can accountants be earth angels? Absolutely. Anyone who has had a great accountant knows how important a caring, focused CPA can be at tax time. I think if someone has the courage to seek out an accountant after avoiding paying their taxes for several years, for example, they need someone who will be not only professional but also compassionate.

The difficult thing about discovering our sensitivity and deepening our spirituality is that many people believe they then have to suddenly upend their whole lives, as if being a professional healer is the only way to heal. There are people with a strong healer archetype in every profession, and that includes the financial and business sectors. These are industries that also need healing, full of institutions and people who could benefit from healing energy. You can fulfill the collective part of your destiny as an earth angel in countless ways that have nothing to do with a profession. Simply being kind and helpful when you can is all that is necessary.

If you feel called to explore changing your profession, or get a side hustle that you feel represents you more authentically than your nine-to-five, that's wonderful. I like to believe that when we are living our purpose, the universe will support us. That is one way I was able to step out in faith and become a professional intuitive and author. However, since we are *earth* angels, we have to remember that our earthly needs must always be considered.

In my case, this meant keeping a full-time job while I spent years working up my side hustle. I only made the jump when I had an amount of savings in the bank that made me feel comfortable leaving my job and enough clients or flow to know I could count on a certain amount of income every month. You might be different and have different needs—you may not be as concerned about savings or you may be in a job you feel you have to leave right now. Just remember that your destiny may ask you to rise to the occasion and overcome many challenges—in fact, most certainly it will—yet thankfully for the average person, your destiny doesn't ask you to put your well-being at risk.

But know that the main thing earth angels need regarding a career or role like full-time caregiver or parent is to simply feel like they can put their heart into what they are doing. This is why I think earth angels make great cashiers or baristas. Sometimes just a smile and a couple of kind words can change a customer's whole day.

Earth angels like to feel like they are on purpose, because having meaning in their lives is very important (as it is to many other people). Find more ways you can create meaning for yourself in the jobs and roles you already hold, whether that's simply being a more present friend or being more considerate to customer service people you interact with on the phone. As an earth angel, never underestimate how much you already give to those around you; it probably comes naturally to you as part of your earth angel destiny.

The Earth Angel Code of Honor

Earth angels tend to have a strong moral compass and dislike injustice; instead, they prefer to act out of a place of honor. When

I asked my celestial angels for a way to sum up the earth angel code of honor, I heard this in reply: "Doing what is best, even when it doesn't personally serve you." In this way, earth angels acknowledge that everyone is connected in some mystical way. So trying to do right by someone else is doing right by yourself too. The earth angel honor code in action could be as simple as encouraging someone you manage to go after a promotion to a different department, even though it will mean you have to spend extra time finding and training their replacement. Or it could be as complex as wanting what is best for your partner, even if what is best for them is to leave the marriage. It could be very easy to live up to the earth angel code of honor, or it could be very painful.

Some days you might ace this honor test, and other days completely bomb. It's not about holding yourself to impossible standards. But try to keep coming back to that code of honor, to do what is best even if it does not personally serve you. This code of honor can be employed for issues in your personal life or global issues. There may be no immediate benefit to you personally to allow someone refugee status in your country, for example, but you might search your heart and consult your head and feel it's the best decision anyway.

I've felt for some time that what you stand for and how you treat others is all you really have at the end of the day. And it can bring you some wonderful karma. Like in the case of a friend of my family who was looking for a job years ago. This person, whom we'll call Chuck, was still young and starting out in his career, and having a terrible time finding a foothold in his industry. An old friend of Chuck's father told him to come down to his office and meet him for lunch. The man explained that he did not have an opening in his company right now, but he wanted to meet Chuck and shake hands.

When Chuck arrived at this man's office, there were a bunch of other people in the large waiting room. One gentleman started loudly badmouthing someone who wasn't there. Chuck recognized the name of the man who was being badmouthed—he didn't know him well, but lots of people in the industry were in this waiting room and listening. The man doing the badmouthing was a big player in the industry. Chuck realized he might be burning a bridge yet he stood up in the waiting room and said, "Hey, I don't appreciate having to sit here and listen to you talk badly about that person. It doesn't seem right to me."

Well, guess who was walking down the hall, out of his office, and into the waiting room at that exact moment? That friend of Chuck's father, who heard the whole exchange. At lunch, he told Chuck that he admired Chuck's sense of honor, and that even though there was no position open right now at his company, he'd make one for Chuck.

This code of honor isn't around to help you judge yourself or others. Please don't fall into that trap. It's simply a guidepost for you to use as a reference, or something to keep coming back to when you need an ethical tune-up.

Trusting Your Journey as an Earth Angel

The going can get rough—and confusing—here on earth. One wonderful thing about being an earth angel is that even when you are confused about your personal destiny (where should I go, what should I do, whom should I partner with) you can always fall back on your collective earth angel destiny to help get your bearings and find direction. That part of your destiny is to be a light for others, a nurturing port of compassion and support and love. Whether you live that out as waitstaff at a restaurant who smiles and brightens the days of your customers, as a parent who guides a child, or as a CEO who gives their employees the best benefits around, what a fabulous destiny you have.

Trusting your journey means trusting that Spirit is real and somehow supporting you as you support others. Lean into your collective earth angel destiny, and see how that helps you feel even more confident that Spirit has your back. You might see evidence of this in grace moments that show up in your life, like people or opportunities or resources that appear right when you need them. Remember that your personal destiny is always changing and evolving. Listen to your heart, which contains the soul's memory, and trust that where it leads you is where you need to be.

If you have trouble trusting your journey, or you look up and just cannot see the path forward regarding your personal destiny, lean into your connection to Spirit and divine angels. Write a journal entry to the universe and ask for some signs about your next best steps. There is always a path ahead for you, earth angel, and if your own light feels a little too dim at the moment to shine the way forward, rely on Spirit to do that for you.

Taking on the Weight of the World Will Break Your Wings

When I was growing up, I was very sensitive. I got my mom's credit card and donated so much money to PETA in junior high that she understandably hit the roof when the bill came but was actually quite sweet about it in the end, and explained to me that as a single mom raising two kids, she could not afford to donate that much. I remember eating peas one night at the table and moving them all closer together so the stray peas would not be lonely. The next day my mom caught me carefully placing two old grapefruit halves face up in the trash, because I just thought they would be happier face up. Growing up as an earth angel and trying to navigate or manage this sensitivity with no road map was not always fun. It's one reason that if parents think they have a sensitive child in the house, they should take note. Reading up on helping a child understand and manage their sensitivity can be the best gift a parent could ever offer a sensitive child.

As I got older, I became really into causes—in high school I was known for this. Save the planet, save the children, shut down the nuclear plants, and so on. The music I listened to and books I read were very socially conscious and political as well. I once met up with a friend from high school when we were both in college, after having not connected with each other in a few years. He asked me what causes I was into at the moment. "Nothing, really," I replied. He looked at me in total shock. "But that's such a big part of who you are!" It's funny how people who love us and know us well can remind us who we really are, on a soul level. By graduate school, I was back to caring very much about what was going on in the larger world around me, and it's still how I am today.

As an earth angel, you might have a tendency to worry about what is going on in the world, not just what is going on with your aunt Elizabeth. You probably worry about people and animals you see on the news who are suffering. You might worry about climate change, pollution, natural resources, and the future of the planet. If you are sensitive, you can create boundaries by simply taking a break from the news or only scanning the headlines. Only allowing yourself so long to think about and feel into the suffering of others is also a useful technique.

Unfortunately, as an earth angel you cannot save or help everyone. This is yet another thing that divine angels and earth angels have in common—the impulse to want to ease the suffering of all people, while being limited in the capacity to do so. As you know from personal experience, divine angels cannot just fly in and save you or your loved ones from suffering—sometimes profound suffering. Yet just like earth angels, divine angels hate to see suffering and want to help you as much as they are able.

Sensitive people might also pick up on the collective emotional current without even thinking about an event or reading about it. When I lived in New York City and something devastating happened, whether it was a natural disaster or an act of terror, I could always feel so clearly the "mood on the street." I went about my normal life during these times and it did not keep me isolated. But it was always helpful to be a little mindful of the fact that as someone who is sensitive, I was able to catch a whiff of the mood on the street. Catching a whiff is one thing. It's another thing to swirl it around in a wine glass and deeply inhale. This is where our focus matters as far as protecting sensitivity. I would try to register or take note of the mood on the street, and then come home to my own energy, wrapping it snuggly around me like a blanket.

I lived in New York City for twenty years, and I would often hear people who would visit say that sensitive people could not survive in a city of that size. For me, I think living in the Big Apple (and I lived *right* on the island of Manhattan in a busy business and tourist district) taught me how and when to tune out. I actually believe New York City taught me to better manage my sensitivity. You learn to go into your own world on a subway car, for instance—listening to your music or reading your book or concentrating on your thoughts—instead of tuning in to the strangers around you.

You'll find the geographic location that best works for you, or you probably already have. I know an earth angel who lives in a rural community and feels she needs that space and immediate, constant contact with nature. Yet I also know earth angels who live in the heart of Paris, and feel they need that bustling, cosmopolitan energy.

As an earth angel it makes sense that world events, or events in your community—even if they are affecting people you don't know and maybe have nothing in common with—upset you. When you find this happening, know that it's because you are being triggered in your collective mission as an earth angel. You came here to help and support those who are struggling, and here you are confronted with a bunch of them on the news. It's like how some dogs instinctively go after birds and squirrels, even though their masters never trained them to hunt. It's something deeper that is triggered or activated in the dog when that squirrel scurries by.

When something is happening in the world and you think it's unfair or feel deeply for those suffering, stop and ground yourself with a few breaths. Move away from the story you are reading and remind yourself that this is affecting you very deeply because as a sensitive person, you really are feeling some of the pain of this situation in your own system. Once you feel grounded in your own energy again, ask yourself if there is anything you can do. Can you post about the situation on social media? Can you make a one-time or recurring donation? Can you change something about your lifestyle or purchasing habits that will help? Could you actually take a week's vacation and go physically volunteer? Can you stop and send a prayer to those who are suffering, or spend a few minutes in meditation sending them healing?

I spoke about praying for strangers in my book *Angel Insights*. Like everyone else, I have definitely read stories in the news or heard about friends of friends who were going through something just awful. Almost unthinkably awful. Whenever this event or person would come to my mind, I would stop and say a quick prayer for them.

I remember once my grandma was in the hospital and everyone was praying for her. "I could feel it," she told me later. I giggled just because we always laughed together, but she got very serious and repeated, "No, Tanya, I mean I really could feel it. Those prayers helped me." Never underestimate the power of a good action step, but also don't underestimate the power of prayer. As a powerful spiritual being (all humans are) your prayers activate something equally powerful in the universe, whether you are praying for yourself or someone else.

You might be an earth angel who feels called to be an activist and work for major shifts in the larger world. Whatever role you play, earth angels taking some kind of action when they see something upsetting in the world can change the world. The trick is to keep your center and always return to your own personal reality and emotional skin. When you encounter suffering, whether it's down the street or across the world, acknowledge it, take action, and then come home to yourself—to your own needs and self-care.

People Like to Open Up and Tell Earth Angels Stuff

I already told you about when I worked at a company and had an office with a door and coworkers were always coming inside to confide in me. Well, this pattern started much earlier. In high school, I always had a long list of people to return calls to. This was before the days of the cell phone and it was rare to give teenagers their own landline, so my stepmother had the thankless duty of taking all my messages. Whether it was a good friend calling to tell me about their problems at home or someone in one of my classes calling for advice about how to ask out one of my friends, people sought me out and told me stuff. "Why are all these people calling you?" my stepmother finally said one day. I didn't have an answer to that question, but I did know that I had hours worth of phone calls to return every day—and somehow it didn't ever occur to me to tell people I couldn't talk or diplomatically give them a time limit when I did call them back. Many teenagers are notorious for talking on the phone, yet it seemed I was someone people wanted to open up to in a significant way.

This continued into my adult life. At a party in my late twenties, I remember talking to a young man there for two hours while he told me all about the issues in his family. At the end he said, "I'm sorry, I don't know why I'm telling you all this." I didn't know him before the party and never saw him again, yet I knew all the intimate details of his immediate family members' lives. Over the years I got used to people telling me, someone they just met at a social gathering, sensitive information that would usually been considered "classified." Now, many times friends or clients will say, "I've never told anyone that before" after opening up and sharing. I used to joke that it was my natural "Irish charm" that brought on these confessions, but now I have the answer to my stepmother's question, "Why are all these people calling you?" I'm an earth angel, and by nature I'm non-judgmental and compassionate. This makes people feel safe to open up and tell earth angels things, knowing earth angels will not pass judgment on the person opening up or anyone else in their story. When you open up to an earth angel, you can usually count on being met with a warm, welcoming, understanding energy. Meeting people with this energy when they share challenging experiences or emotions is part of an earth angel's destiny.

People who know me well might say that I can be judgmental, all right. I have very strong opinions on politics and culture, and when someone wrongs me or someone I love personally, of course, I can be judgmental. What I'm referring to are those times I'm anchored into my earth angel energy, when a client or friend or stranger is sharing with me something about their life that I have nothing to do with or no personal stake in.

Mercy and compassion help us be nonjudgmental, and as an earth angel just know that you might feel very judgmental to people who have wronged you personally. That's natural. But I bet you are the kind of person that holds an open, compassionate, merciful space for people in your life when they need to get something off their chest. Sometimes telling someone else that it's okay, that they shouldn't judge themselves so harshly, that they should consider forgiving themselves is all another person needs to hear to view themselves and their circumstances in a much more compassionate way. This can flick a switch in someone's mind and have a profound effect on their ability to move on from a trauma or encourage them to love themselves through it.

You can encourage people to hold themselves accountable while still treating themselves with mercy—the two are not mutually exclusive. Being a compassionate earth angel does not mean being an enabler either. You can listen with love and still suggest someone make healthy changes.

If people seek you out for advice or as someone to listen to them with a loving earth angel energy, try to make time for this. In the case of strangers, they might just be sensing your earth angel energy before you have said anything to give your compassionate nature away. You will have to put boundaries around it, just like I eventually had to do in high school and college with my friends so I could get some homework done. Now talking on the phone to people all over the world is my job, and you might have a similar professional role where you listen to people. No matter what you do in the world, know that as a nurturing earth angel you are a natural listener and confidante.

Seeing Things from All Sides While Still Honoring Your Needs

Earth angels seem to have a unique ability to see things from all sides of an issue. That's because as sensitive people, earth angels can actually tune in to another person's experience of a situation. This is why earth angels can be wonderful diplomats at the office or in their families. They can step into a situation and help mediate, especially if they happen to be very good communicators.

As an earth angel you might have found yourself mediating between fellow colleagues who see the same situation very differently, or mediating between family members who rub each other the wrong way. You might remind your cousin that your aunt can have intense emotional reactions to things but then calms down after a day or two, while you assure your aunt that your cousin didn't mean to say something thoughtless—she just has a sarcastic sense of humor. You may even find yourself jumping in to mediate situations between people you don't know at all, like a barista and a fellow customer when there is confusion about an order.

It's wonderful that earth angels can see things from all sides—it makes them more compassionate people and the universe knows we can always use more compassion on earth, especially in situations where people are upset and triggered. This is part of an earth angel's greater collective destiny. Yet earth angels need to remember that after they have used their feelers to tune in to the people around them and see the situation from the other perspectives, earth angels must return to their own emotional skin and their own personal perspective—which might have evolved a little after getting all those other perspectives. Earth angels must always keep returning home to their own needs. That is part of your destiny as well—to honor your own experience. I had a client once who found himself in a situation that illustrates this perfectly. We'll call him John.

John loved cars. He got such a thrill out of driving them and having all the fun gadgets and comparing the styles and colors. After going without a car or driving cars that were a little beaten up and decades old for his whole life, John found himself in the position to buy a new car—brand new. He got so much joy out of simply running errands—opening the sun roof, turning on the radio, and enjoying how the car handled on the road.

After having the car for two months, with the dealer tags still on it, John was rear-ended. When the other driver got out of their car to talk, my client noticed how shaken up the young woman who rear-ended him was. Being an earth angel, John immediately went into the mode of comforting *her*, even though the smash had already caused some soreness in his body and sent coffee flying all over his new interior. "I've never been in a wreck before," the woman said. "I'm sorry. I wasn't paying close enough attention. This is my company's car and I was just coming from a job site. I only got this job a few weeks ago."

They exchanged insurance and contact information, my earth angel client assuring the young woman that the damage looked minimal and they would work something out. "I realized later that all I was concerned about was comforting and reassuring her," John said. "I probably should not have said that the damage was minimal, since I didn't really know." When my client took the car to the dealership, they told him the bumper was cracked and that a couple of the sensors were damaged and would need to be replaced. Either the woman's company insurance would have to pay or John and the woman who hit him would have to come to an arrangement.

My client called his insurance to find out his options, and reminded himself that the important thing was that no one was hurt. Anyone reading this who has been injured in a car wreck or even lost a loved one in a car wreck knows that is really all that matters—everyone was safe. John called the woman on the phone to let her know the situation, that there was in fact some damage that would need to be seen to. "Oh, my God. I just pray I don't get fired for this! I would pay for the damages myself, but that's all the money I have in the bank right now. I'm so sorry. I'll have to tell my boss what happened and hope for the best." Turns out this was the woman's first job out of college, she had student loans to repay, and it had taken her a whole year to find this job.

When my client hung up the phone, he felt so badly for the woman that he actually considered letting the whole thing go, even though it would cost him thousands of dollars out of pocket, or increase his insurance premiums if he filed a claim with his insurance. At first he came up with some numbers that the company could pay that would cover the cost that seemed reasonable and in line with the estimate he had received. "But what about the value of your car?" a friend told him. "Do you realize that once a car has been in a wreck and had bodywork done, the value of that car goes down significantly? Because this woman rear-ended you, if you ever wanted to sell that car you will get so much less. Whatever deal you come to with this company or their insurance, it has to take into account the value of the car."

"God, you're right," John said. "But I hate to tell her the figure is much higher than I thought."

"Quit being such a nice guy," his friend said. "This is how you get taken advantage of."

My client sat with all the information—his side of things (he had a brand-new car that he was making monthly payments on that was now majorly devalued, yet he did not want to ruin this young woman's life over one mistake), the perspective of the woman who hit him (she had never been in a wreck before, had made a mistake, was living paycheck to paycheck as many Americans do, and feared her boss's reaction), and his good friend's perspective (you have to stand up for yourself or you will get taken advantage of).

All of these perspectives were valid. Yet John had to come home to himself and honor his instincts. He could distill his needs down to two major points: Since the accident was in no way his fault, he needed to be compensated for the damages both to the car and its value. Secondly, he wanted to cause this young woman as little pain as possible. He felt that while some things in life might be random accidents, he believed this one was not. Once he used his feelers to tune in to the situation, he realized that the woman was a young driver and maybe needed to learn a lesson about paying closer attention while she was behind the wheel. Also, the fact that she hit an earth angel meant that she would be treated with as much compassion as possible during this process.

The woman who hit John was also his teacher, showing him that he had to still stand up for his own needs and perspective while being a compassionate earth angel. When he felt into the situation for further spiritual perspectives, he decided the accident forced him to slow down. He was in the middle of looking for his first home to purchase, and after the accident he realized he wanted to just get used to the debt of a new car for a bit before adding a mortgage on top.

In the end, John spoke to the woman's boss and assured her that this worker had behaved kindly and responsibly to him since the accident, and that he hoped she would not be let go because of this one mistake. In this way my client honored his earth angel destiny, to promote healing and compassion. The young woman who hit my client emailed him months later to say that she did not lose her job, but the anxiety she already suffered from got a bit worse after the accident. This led her to get some help for that, something she knew she needed but had been putting off. So this particular car accident had been a powerful lesson for these two humans. Since no one was injured and no one's life was altered, except in positive ways, these lessons felt worth it and were met with peace and gratitude. This fender bender taught the young woman to be very careful and alert while on the road, which will keep her and everyone else safer.

Earth Angel Exercise

Coming Back Home to Yourself after Considering the Perspectives of Others

Look through these steps and consider each one carefully the next time you find yourself an earth angel in a difficult situation like John who was rear-ended:

Step 1. Take time to decide how you want to act.

If at all possible, take some time to mull things over before you decide what your position will be on this issue. You might have strong initial emotional reactions about your perspective or other people's, or you might initially reject some good advice that days later seems like divine guidance (sometimes Spirit will speak to you by putting in the mind of a loved one or even a stranger an important perspective that you need to hear). It's always ideal to take a few days, or at least a few hours, to process, let things settle, and connect with your intuition about next best steps. This allows you time to consider everything, get your emotions processed to a degree, and come home to yourself.

Step 2. Consider the spiritual perspective(s).

This is something my client asked himself about the car accident—was there a greater reason why this happened? Even if it does not seem like the event was pre-destined, and certainly I think many times it can be a case of things simply happening in the moment, Spirit will immediately get on the scene to offer people grace and also some chances for growth. Does it seem like there are any lessons or chances for spiritual growth for you or other people in this situation? You might not only observe these realizations but factor them into your opinion of the situation and how you will take action going forward. If the situation was very devastating, give yourself space to process your challenging emotions like grief or anger before attempting to consider a spiritual perspective.

Step 3. Factor in past wounds.

It's possible that a current challenging event will trigger a past wound. In the example we just read about my client getting into a fender bender, if either of them had ever been in a traumatic car wreck where someone was seriously injured or there were significant consequences to the person responsible, this wreck would have surely triggered those old wounds. When old wounds are triggered, we usually have a much stronger, more emotional, and possibly even inappropriate reaction to an event. Often we do not realize a past trauma has been activated until we sit down and ask ourselves if this could be the case. So whenever you have a really intense reaction to something, and you feel like your reaction might be out of step with the situation or over-the-top, get quiet and ask yourself if there has been an old wound triggered by this current situation. It could be an old wound from last year or from decades ago. It might even be an old wound from another lifetime. And bear in mind the wound might be one you consider huge or minor. Either way, if it's affecting how you are processing this situation it's worth paying attention to. The wound might be crying out for a new level of care and healing.

Step 4. Don't abandon your earth angel mission, but don't abandon yourself either.

It's okay to want to be kind and compassionate toward others when dealing with challenging situations. That's part of why you came to earth, to tune in to others and see how you can help. There will always be vast differences in situations about how kind and generous you can be, but find some way to honor your earth angel energy in every situation. It's an important part of you, and you'll feel more peaceful about the situation in the long run if you get the chance to act like an earth angel in some way. Just remember that your needs are as important as anyone else's, and often the only person who will stand up for your needs and perspective in a situation is you.

Handling an Earthly Life That Isn't "Fair"

Many of the earth angels I have worked with as clients or known as colleagues and friends get very worked up about injustice. My mother often reminded me as a child that "life isn't fair." If I got bullied at school or was blamed for something I didn't do or saw an animal suffering, this explanation that life simply was not fair only enraged me further. Yet as I got older, I appreciated this life lesson. Life is not fair. But wanting life to be fair or working to make it more fair for everyone is part of the earth angel collective destiny.

Earth angels might have personal destinies where they have the power to significantly impact the level of fairness on this planet. They might be given a huge public platform where they are able to dramatically influence people to become more compassionate. Or earth angels might be given massive fortunes where they can dramatically improve the quality of people's lives through charity work.

For most of us, we are not able to make such an obviously significant impact within our personal destiny. But never underestimate how you influence others. Maybe a philanthropist was taught the importance of giving back as a child when he watched his poor grandmother put a dollar in the collection plate at church. Or maybe a senator was taught how important equal rights were by their father who was a public school teacher.

Living your collective earth angel destiny about the desire for the world to be more fair could come from marching in a peaceful protest, making a complaint about unfair treatment on the job, or simply standing up to a loved one when you are being treated unfairly. Earth angels might feel very passionate about seeing themselves or others treated unfairly within their family or friend tribes.

When discerning fairness, remember that it can be quite subjective. What feels very unfair to you might seem like proper justice to someone else. Always consider the spiritual perspective, like the example from this chapter of my client who was in a fender bender. Was it fair for the woman who hit him to have to sweat it out? Was it fair that his new car was damaged? Possibly not, but from a spiritual perspective they both grew significantly from the experience, which might have prevented a more serious accident down the line. In that sense, it was very fair.

If something that was extremely unfair happened to you, and there is no spiritual perspective or any other perspective that softens the blow, I am truly sorry from the bottom of my heart. That is one of the graces and challenges of being an earth angel—knowing you came here to try to make things a little more fair in tiny or monumental ways, yet having to come to peace with my mother's wisdom, that life simply is not always fair.

Earth Angels on the Job

I once had a client who had been away on medical leave from her job for several months recovering from an injury. She said people at work were always emailing her, telling her how much her "energy" was missed around the office. Coworkers missed her pep talks, the way she complimented people or cheered them up, and how she went out of her way to make other people's day brighter and more meaningful. Is there anyone at your office like that? They are probably an earth angel.

Another earth angel client had assumed a significant amount of responsibility at the office. She was known as the rock, who could be counted on to see difficult or complex tasks through. This enabled her to earn a good salary and have excellent job security. She was often told by her company that they didn't know how things would get done if she wasn't around, and coworkers were dreading the day she either quit or retired.

You might relate to one or perhaps both of these women. Are you the mother/father or the rock at your place of employment? You might have other earth angel colleagues who also assume these roles. Perhaps you are an earth angel who feels like the Cinderella at work—always toiling away and not receiving the compensation or recognition you feel you deserve.

The common theme with all these earth angel office archetypes—the mother/father, the rock, and Cinderella/victim, is that in each scenario the earth angel is in danger of giving too much and experiencing burnout. Since the earth angel collective destiny is to help and guide others, you probably like giving at work. Maybe working a little harder or giving a little more has always felt good and natural to you. Just have your own back or wings as far as burnout symptoms.

For some earth angels being taken advantage of by a boss or coworker or client might be a little more likely. I remembered years ago hearing a story about a man who had finally realized he was being taken advantage of at work. A colleague was always asking him to help him out at the last minute, because this earth angel was very conscientious and got his work done early. Many sensitive people prefer to hit deadlines well in advance if possible so they avoid the unnecessary stress of feeling into the emotions of others who will be upset or nervous about them hitting the deadline. Other folks find pushing it to the last minute inspiring.

Every month this earth angel would say to his coworker, "Sure, no problem. I'll help you finish your project." This went on for years, to the point that the coworker just stopped even attempting to begin this project every month and simply handed it over straight away to his colleague. Finally, the earth angel doing more than his fair share said, "No, I can't help you this month." The coworker had already dropped the project on the earth angel's desk and was walking away when he heard that, and more: "You've been giving me your work for years, and while I don't mind helping you out occasionally, this pattern we have established has to stop." And stop it did. While his coworker was taken aback by the earth angel's uncharacteristic response, he understood and apologized.

This might sound like an extreme example, but see if you can locate a bit of yourself in this earth angel employee's experience. In my experience both as an intuitive seeing clients and as an employee who had worked nine-to-five positions at companies, I've found that sensitive people are typically very hardworking and truly care about the quality of their work and other people's feelings. This is wonderful, but it can also set sensitive people up for working too hard or caring too much.

An earth angel friend who leads a team of employees at a large company got a huge promotion many years ago. He was thrilled, yet the promotion did not come with added staff—although it did come with added duties. For the first few weeks after the promotion my friend struggled to keep up with his new duties while still doing everything he used to do. "I know now that I need to start delegating some of my old duties out to my team," he said, "but I just wanted to see if I could avoid that." Some managers would have immediately dumped a bunch of stuff on their team without thinking twice. But this gentleman genuinely cared about his team and as a sensitive person could see things from their perspectives. That's why he was the most popular manager at the company and people always tried to transfer to his team.

If you are an earth angel who feels you don't have enough to do, that can be equally problematic. I once had an earth angel client we'll call Beth, whose husband had passed away and left her very comfortably provided for so she did not need to work outside the home. I encouraged Beth to get a part-time job or a volunteer position, but Beth was still grieving the loss of her husband and wasn't sure if she wanted to take on anything more. One day Beth was shopping in her favorite health food store chatting with the owner. "You know so much about these supplements, Beth, you should come work here on Saturdays," the owner said. "I could use the extra help."

Beth took the owner up on her offer, and soon she was working several days a week and helping with the ordering. Beth loved sharing her knowledge and interacting with the customers. As an earth angel, Beth was wired to want to make a positive impact in the lives of others. In Beth's case, having a part-time job was exactly what she needed to help her recover from the trauma of losing her husband. Beth had been a devoted wife, and now she took that energy out in the world and devoted it to the customers and the owner at the health food store.

Earth Angel Exercise
Managing Anticipatory Stress

When I describe anticipatory stress to sensitive clients they always say, "Yeah, that's me." Is the lead-up time to a big or challenging event even worse for you than the event itself? Often sensitive people can almost torture themselves with stress about an event during the lead-up time, and then the talk with their boss or first date or public speech is not at all as stressful or dramatic as they imagined. The anticipation is often the worst part of such situations for sensitive folks.

The hardest part is that a fear of anticipatory stress itself can cause sensitive people to isolate or not take healthy risks like applying for a new job, asking a new friend out for coffee, or trying a new physical activity like yoga. So when we talk about earth angels fulfilling their destinies, getting a handle on anticipatory stress really helps.

The next time you catch yourself suffering from anticipatory stress, whether it's intense or just annoyingly distracting, employ the following techniques.

1. **Prepare ahead of time.** Earth angels are often the type of people who appreciate being prepared, on time, and having their metaphorical ducks in a row. How can you prepare for

this event in a reasonable way to lesson your anticipatory stress?

2. **Use creative visualization to imagine a positive outcome.** You might picture yourself being calm and open as you ask your manager for a promotion, or you could picture yourself telling the person you're dating that you are falling in love with them in a confident, heartfelt manner.

3. **Don't think about the event more than you have to.** Be mindful about how much time you spend on this event ahead of time, even if that time seems productive. Are you double and triple checking things that you know are under control? Have you practiced playing a song or giving a speech so many times that it has become dull or rote and thus might negatively affect your performance?

4. **Spend some of your prep time unwinding and blowing off steam.** This is productive as being relaxed and balanced ahead of time will help you have the same energy during the situation you are anticipating. Sensitive earth angels should emphasize low-stimulation activities to help calm their nervous systems.

Earth Angels Making Peace with Confrontation

Confrontation—the word can seem like kryptonite to some earth angels, making them shrink back and feel weak or powerless. Yet your ability to handle confrontation in a healthy way has a direct effect on the quality of your life, and most certainly a direct effect on your career and your destiny. If your career or calling is being a full-time parent, you know that there are many moments you need to be assertive about confrontation, not just with your kids but with other parents, teachers, healthcare providers, etc.

When you avoid confrontation it can make a bad situation worse. If a client leaves you a voicemail that they are unhappy with the work you are doing on their home (this might be interior decorating, landscaping, or remodeling) and your immediate instinct is to avoid them and hide under the bed, it might be your sensitivity shrinking back from having to engage in a confrontation where their upset emotions register deeply in your own system. It doesn't mean you are a coward that you put off having this necessary conversation, it's simply that you are sensitive.

Part of successful confrontation as an earth angel is acknowledging that confrontation can really trigger your sensitivity. After a disagreement with a coworker you might find your heart racing and your hands shaking. Even public speaking is a kind of confrontation, where you are confronting a large audience of people. You might have a friend who also had a public speaking gig on the same day you did, or who also had a tough talk with a coworker on the same afternoon, yet by the evening your friend has totally calmed down. Their nervous system feels relaxed and they have kind of moved on from the stress or anxiety of the moment. Meanwhile the day after the same type of event you are still keyed up. The difference in your reactions is probably that you are sensitive and your friend is not, or at least not as sensitive as you.

Confrontation usually, though not always, involves some strong emotions. It can also require the courage to work yourself up to speak your mind, like if you're having a company meeting and everyone else is psyched about a new project coming in but you already see some red flags and feel the need to inform the group (sensitive people are often very good at anticipating problematic issues that others can miss). Because sensitive people can pick up more easily on even subtle stimuli, you will obviously pick up even more on strong emotions too.

We have already discussed anticipatory stress, and this is certainly something that sensitive people can experience before a confrontation. This anticipatory stress could make them more prone to avoiding or sidestepping confrontation. Yet often anticipatory stress is the worst part of the confrontation. Many times I have had sensitive clients tell me they dreaded a talk with a business partner and then when they were actually engaged in the confrontation found that it was not nearly as bad as they had anticipated. This can leave sensitive people feeling a bit foolish, like they had tortured themselves for days ahead of time only to feel much relief after the confrontation.

Getting better at managing confrontation will improve not only your career but every area of your life. If you realize you are still keyed up after a confrontation even when things went relatively smoothly, remind yourself that your sensitive system is simply still overstimulated. It's a technical issue you are temporarily having. Engage in some nurturing low-stimulation downtime to reset.

Earth Angel Exercise
Confrontation Techniques

These might be helpful to prepare for your next confrontation. If you don't have time to prepare, and the confrontation happens on the fly, try to calm and ground yourself afterward to help you recover more quickly. Avoid unnecessary drama after the confrontation.

Step 1. Remind yourself that confrontation is simply a natural part of life.

Humans are going to disagree or have issues with one another from time to time. Normalizing confrontation in your mind either before or after a confrontation should help your nervous system. If confrontation between you and an individual or a group is happening constantly or you seem to be having confrontations with people often, you might want to look more closely at what is behind all this.

Step 2. Ask yourself if you think other people's emotions are your responsibility.

As earth angels who are on a mission of compassion and assistance to other humans, you might have tricked yourself into thinking that other people's emotions are your jurisdiction. Sit with this on a conscious and subconscious level. It would make sense that somewhere inside you at one time or another you believed this since as an earth angel you are empathic and may have confused being able to feel other people's emotions with an obligation to manage them. Whether you are managing the emotions of others in an effort to spare them the emotion or to spare yourself from feeling it in a secondhand way, know that other people have a right to their emotional response. That emotion might be important for them to feel, process, and learn from.

Step 3. Create healthy distance between yourself and the other person by entering into an observer or witnessing mode.

Sensitive people can steel themselves to feel less of the emotional reaction of others during challenging interactions by entering into observer mode or engaging witnessing energy. This is something that you will get better at the more you practice it. Pull back or retract your feelers a bit before you go into a confrontation. You can even think of opening up the psychic pathway called claircognizance, the intellectual psychic pathway, before you enter into a confrontation. This will allow you to observe with more emotional detachment the other person's reaction and position, sort of like watching a movie. While sensitive people might be moved greatly by movies and find that characters really come to life, think of an interesting series you watch just to blow off steam, or a dry documentary or detective drama that makes you think strategically instead of emotionally. Witness the other person that way during the confrontation. It might help you hear them better. Then after the confrontation is over, you can retreat and get your feelers back out to feel into the situation again.

Step 4. Notice your confrontation style, and the confrontation style of the other person.

Odds are you have knocked around the world long enough to have had many confrontations. Think back on them, some of your earliest ones and some of your more recent ones, and see if you can notice a style or any patterns. Do you tend to back down and try to soothe the other person? Do you come in hot before waiting for your emotions to cool? Maybe you are a natural diplomat and feel that calming others down, listening, speaking your truth, and then coming up with action steps or compromises is a real strength. Do you always walk away wishing you had been more honest? Do you prefer to deal with a confrontation right away, or do you like to give it some space first? Is there anything else you would like to change about your confrontation style? Do you know the confrontation style of the other person?

Sometimes it might be best to modify your confrontation style to better suit certain people or situations. If your mate was abandoned by both of her parents, your natural confrontation style of wanting to retreat and then re-enter talks later when you feel ready might be way too triggering for your mate. When you leave a fight "unfinished" to retreat, it mirrors your mate's experiences of being abandoned. In a case like this, you and your mate might come up with a confrontation style as a couple, where some initial conclusion is agreed upon during a confrontation, even if that agreement is temporary, and every confrontation ends with saying, "I love you" or "I'm not going anywhere."

You Are a Powerful Spiritual Being

This is something I am *always* reminding people. Even if you don't feel very powerful right now, or like you have no power at all (and we can all relate to feeling that way), you really are incredibly powerful. This does not mean that you can leap tall buildings in a single bound or suddenly manifest a million dollars into your savings account overnight. But it does mean that as a powerful spiritual being you have the ability to cocreate some part of your journey here on earth.

All humans are powerful spiritual beings. We can forget this because sometimes we feel at the mercy of so many things: the economy, our family of origin, our health problems, our addictions, our past poor choices. But the fact of the matter is you are as powerful as the divine angels who inhabit that dimension called heaven. The earthly experience isn't always a pleasure cruise. Sometimes we really are at the mercy of fated events and other people's free will choices. Yet that does not change your nature as a powerful spiritual being.

As an earth angel, part of how you cocreate your life is through your actions and your energy. You may find yourself in a situation that is less than pleasant—like being in the middle of a divorce, or suddenly moving to a new town where you know no one, or having a doctor give you a scary diagnosis. But there is still a lot of room for you to cocreate, no matter what the circumstances you are facing.

Every day we are given many chances to cocreate our reality both in the moment and in the future regarding the seeds we plant that later come to harvest. The following can be a wonderful question to ask yourself as you get ready for the day, like while you are in the shower, on your commute, or eating breakfast: "What will be my cocreative opportunities for the day? And what am I trying to cocreate in my life today?" Answers might be a more peaceful mind, a more harmonious romantic relationship, a healthier body, a simpler lifestyle, a fulfilling creative project, a feeling of increased abundance, or chances to express your earth angel-ness in the world.

A Final Note on Earth Angels and Destiny

Being an earth angel is an important and very rewarding part of your destiny. Just how much you want to live in that earth angel destiny every day is up to you. Keep in mind that being there for others can be as simple as offering them a smile or saying "please" and "thank you." In the hustle and bustle of modern life, we sometimes lose track of simple heart-centered interactions. These are moments where earth angels can shine. Part of the reason you want to devote yourself to your earth angel destiny in both large and small ways is because of the wonderful feeling it gives you. Being good to others is how earth angels are good to themselves.

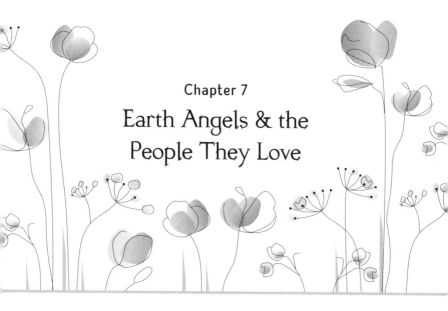

Chapter 7

Earth Angels & the People They Love

As synchronicity would have it, I began writing this chapter of the book at the very beginning of February. The store windows were already decorated with luscious red hearts, and every morning my inbox was full of gift ideas for Valentine's Day. I always get excited this time of year because I love celebrating Galentine's Day on February 13th, an unofficial holiday that is growing in popularity. Begun as a gag on a tv show, many women now feel that a day of "ladies celebrating ladies" should be a real thing.

Earth angels of all genders and gender identifications can appreciate the notion of celebrating friendships, because close friendships, whether they are with fellow earth angels or other fabulous humans, are so precious to tender-hearted earth angels. So while this chapter does cover romantic love, I just wanted to take a moment to say how important friendships are to all humans. With sensitive earth angels, close friendships can be deeply nourishing and sustaining.

If you're an earth angel, no matter what time of year you are reading this book, take a moment to send a dear friend a small care package in the mail or send them an email letting them know how much their friendship means. If you've been feeling lonely, look into volunteer opportunities or spiritual communities where you might find other like-minded earth angels to bond with. I'd like to thank all of the friends I've been blessed with over the years, the ones I knew when I was very young, the ones who support me so well now, and the ones to come in the future.

Here's to love—loving other people and being loved in return.

Earth Angels and Emotional Family Dynamics

Elizabeth Bennett from *Pride & Prejudice* is hands down the most popular Jane Austen heroine. But *my* favorite Austen lady is also one of my favorite fictional earth angels—Elinor Dashwood from Jane Austen's famous novel *Sense & Sensibility*. If you haven't read the book, there are some delightful film and tv adaptations, most notably the 2008 BBC miniseries and Emma Thompson's 1995 Oscar-winning film adaptation. The story, set in early 1800s England, begins with the death of Elinor's father, which leaves her mother and two younger sisters grieving the loss of someone they loved dearly. It also leaves these four women in a financially precarious position, as their older brother by a previous marriage is set to inherit the family home and fortune.

Families are always quirky, and Elinor's is no different. Elinor's mother and two sisters each have their own challenging emotional reactions to this situation—they cry, yell, or—in the case of the youngest daughter—hide. Meanwhile Elinor is very concerned for the feelings of others, even—despite the fact she was born to a wealthy and aristocratic family—the feelings of her servants and how the transition will affect their lives. While Elinor has her own challenging emotions about the death of her father and the loss of financial stability, she chooses to process these emotions, for the most part, internally.

Elinor helps her sisters and mother navigate their new normal, taking on the role of rock in the family in practical ways by looking for an affordable new place to live. She becomes the emotional guardian too by acting as a diplomat and buffer between the emotionally raw and expressive women in her family and the members of her brother's family when they arrive to take ownership of the family estate. As an earth angel, Elinor naturally becomes concerned with trying help everyone else have a smoother journey.

Is Elinor, or any other real-life earth angel like her, destined to become a martyr in a larger family system? Not at all. But Elinor's instinct to put her own emotional needs aside and run around tending to the needs of everyone around her is very much a natural impulse of sensitive people, especially earth angels. Not only can earth angels sense all the intense emotions in a room, but they genuinely want people to feel better because they are so service-oriented. So in many ways, Elinor is on mission as an earth angel and her gifts shine in a crisis like this—when those around her are struggling and need extra practical and emotional support.

You might have loved ones who occasionally need more support from you, like a young adult who is applying for colleges or trade schools and needs your practical help vetting institutions or filling out financial aid applications. Or maybe you have a sister in another state with a health challenge and you enjoy touching in with her on the phone regularly to listen and offer love. Perhaps you find yourself feeling contented and purposeful in the role of support, so that even when you walk away from someone needy or in crisis, knowing you alleviated their suffering, if only to a degree or only temporarily, leaves you with a deep sense of peace and accomplishment. That amazing feeling you get after supporting a loved one is simply your earth angel energy activating and doing what it so longs for.

What should you watch out for as far as being an earth angel in a larger family dynamic? As Jane Austen's story progresses, Elinor falls in love and, if she were alive and in the modern world on Facebook, her relationship status would say, "it's complicated." Her middle sister, Marianne, is also in love; unlike Marianne, Elinor keeps her cards very close to her chest. At several points Marianne, who is more emotionally intense and needs to process her feelings by expressing them openly to the world, accuses her sister Elinor of not feeling as deeply. This is ironic, since Elinor is incredibly sensitive and as an earth angel feels not only her own emotions acutely but also the emotions of everyone else in the immediate vicinity. One day Elinor explodes on Marianne, reacting in anger to this accusation of being cold yet also pouring her heart out about all she has been keeping in. This earth angel can stop being strong for everyone else and just be honest and vulnerable about her own internal emotional experience.

Why do earth angels sometimes downplay their own emotional experience to partners and loved ones? Earth angels can tend to downplay a lot of things, and generally pretend that whatever is going on with them is not as bad as it seems. We might look to the earth angel's natural optimism to explain some of this phenomenon—an inclination to always look on the bright side. In part, earth angels also downplay things in an effort to protect those around them. If an earth angel is in recovery from addiction, her instinct might be to downplay how challenging the initial weeks and months of recovery are to friends and family so as not to worry them. Yet earth angels also downplay as a way to protect themselves.

If you are a sensitive person, it might seem bad enough to have to face all the challenging emotions that come with a difficult situation without having to feel the challenging emotions of everyone else's concern for you (or any stress your situation causes them). If the challenging situation isn't happening to you, it could still be a recipe for downplaying. You might be an earth angel who has a partner who is out of work or struggling in some way with their career. There may not seem to be room for you to share your emotional experience about this situation with your partner—perhaps it has caused financial hardships for the whole family. You may find that adding your own emotional challenges to the mix by expressing them openly is an extra challenge.

If you love to support the loved ones in your life, it does not necessarily mean there is any kind of unhealthy dynamic at play. You might just be an earth angel doing what earth angels love to do—and do best. Just make sure you create space for your own emotional experience. Whether this is setting aside time to journal about your feelings, putting on your favorite sappy album and having a cry about your situation, or talking to a friend or counselor. It's important that an earth angel's family see them holistically—challenging emotions and all. In some ways and at some times, you need to let loved ones know what is really going on with you.

Toward the end of Jane Austen's story, Elinor has to decide whether or not she will help someone else—even though it's the right thing to do, helping means it will cause Elinor great pain…what do you think she decides? Earth angels typically want the best for other people, even if what is best for them will hurt an earth angel. This might look like encouraging your sibling and roommate to get married, even though it will be lonelier for you around the house after they have moved out. But don't worry, Elinor has a happy ending and lots of blessings by the finish of the book. Everyone, including earth angels, deserves this.

Earth Angels' Boundaries with Family Members

Part of a family seeing an earth angel holistically is realizing that the earth angel is different in specific ways from other members of the family. We're all different, unique, worthy, and special, and earth angels' family members should realize that their earth angels are wired to give, be compassionate, and actually crave supporting others.

Here's a typical example: Dale and Shawn are partners who both work from home in different industries. One Sunday Dale wakes up and thinks, "What a wonderful Sunday! I'm going to give myself an oracle card reading on the porch with my new angel deck. After a big breakfast, I'll do a little work on my creative writing project." Dale hadn't had time to work on that hobby project lately and was looking forward to getting back to the characters he was creating. Dale knew that even though it was Sunday this was a crunch day for his partner, Shawn, who had an urgent freelance project come in the night before.

Dale left Shawn alone in his office, but then an hour later, just as Dale was finishing his oracle reading for himself on the porch, Shawn burst in. "I need your help!" he said. "I'm so nervous about impressing this client that I cannot think straight."

Dale began putting his oracle cards away, seeing his whole lazy, fun Sunday evaporate. Yet he could also see how worked up his partner was and that he needed Dale's help. "Don't worry," Dale told Shawn. "My day is pretty open. I'm happy to help." Dale spent the next five hours helping Shawn put together his presentation PDF for the client. But it was all worth it at the end when Shawn gave Dale a big hug and told him how great the PDF looked. "I love you so much," Shawn said. "I don't know what I would do without you." Dale lived to hear stuff like this, and the feeling of satisfaction he always got after coming through for someone when they really needed it. By the time Dale looked up at the clock it was evening. Dale didn't mention how Shawn's request had derailed his day…he didn't want to hurt Shawn's feelings.

The next morning, Monday, Dale wanted to work at his favorite bookstore café. He'd mentioned to Shawn several times over the past few days that he would need a ride there and then a ride home five hours later. Dale and Shawn had scaled back to one car so they could use the extra money to pay off their home quicker. Their favorite grocery store was a short walk from the bookstore, so as Dale hopped out of the car when they arrived, he called to Shawn, "I'll pick up some things at the store after I'm done and you can grab me there." They decided to rendezvous at 3:30 in the grocery store parking lot, but around 2:00 Dale got an annoyed text from Shawn: "This whole thing of you going to the bookstore to work today is really cutting into my work. Can I pick you up at 2:30 instead of 3:30?" Dale had just taken a seat in the outdoor section of the grocery store with a salad. He texted Shawn back, "Okay, I'll eat my salad as fast as I can and get the shopping done quickly." Dale normally loved to linger over his salad but made fast work of it and then hit the aisles with a cart…wasn't Shawn out of his favorite healthy cereal? He'd grab that and Mother's Day cards for each of their moms.

When Dale met Shawn in the parking lot, Shawn said, "Dale, it's been a bit of a hassle shuttling you to and from the bookstore café when you really didn't need to go there." Dale was dumbstruck for a moment, realizing that this had taken approximately forty minutes out of Shawn's day, round trip, when Dale had spent five hours helping Shawn with his presentation just yesterday. When Dale pointed this out, Shawn said, "But you told me you were happy to help and that your day was pretty open."

Dale just rolled his eyes as he put the bags in the trunk. "I got a card for your mother and a box of your favorite cereal."

It's tempting to see Shawn as the bad guy here, but perhaps there isn't a bad guy—just two very different guys who are not communicating well. Shawn is right, Dale did make it seem like he was happy to help. He'd also never told Shawn that he did some of his best work at that bookstore café, and that enjoying a salad outside the grocery store was a treat he looked forward to all week. Dale is the earth angel in the family, often looking to be supportive and nurturing—and processing some of his challenging emotions internally. Shawn brings the entertainment—he is a very smart, funny, high energy person whose friends and projects are fascinating. Shawn is also very emotionally intense and expressive (so Dale often hears how much he is loved and appreciated). But with an earth angel in the house, Shawn has to be aware that his partner might at times give too much or not be as honest about his emotional experience if it's contradictory to Shawn's. As an earth angel, Dale loves to be supportive. But Dale also needs to speak up for himself so he does not take on the role of victim or martyr.

Sometimes workplaces can feel like families—with all the quirkiness, love, and dysfunction associated with families. You might be an earth angel in the middle of a chain of command that includes a manager above you and someone you manage below you. Part of your personal process as a manager might be getting to know the person you are managing and using your feelers to see if the person you manage is thriving and happy in the position or is frustrated with any part of it. While this is still business, as an earth angel you cannot help but want to facilitate a good experience for your employee and you have created an open environment where you encourage this person you manage to come to you for help whenever they are having trouble.

Your manager's style is very different from yours. She is a no-nonsense person who is very bottom-line oriented. If things are running smoothly with no problems, she is happy. If not, she will be in your face to troubleshoot the issue. Your happiness or personal life does not seem to factor into it with her. It's all about the product or service at the end and if it's up to snuff. This is a job, after all, she might say, *not* a group therapy session.

There may not be anything wrong with either your managing style or your boss's—although ideally you could both take a page from the other's book. As an earth angel, it's natural that you want to bond with the people around you and create a holistic dynamic with them. Just be careful that you aren't so concerned with your employee's experience that you neglect what is best for you—or your employee's performance. That is a mistake your boss would never make.

Part of understanding and making the most of your role in any family—whether it's a family you were born into, a work family you were hired into, or a friend family you chose to enter—is remembering that you are an earth angel.

Not Letting Other People Make Your Decisions for You

Because earth angels can try to avoid conflict and slip into people pleasing, they can also fall into letting life happen to them and taking a back seat to some of the minor and major decisions of their life. This could look like letting a parent decide what your career will be or letting a partner decide where you live. It might be more minor decisions, like letting a child decide their own bedtime or letting a coworker decide that they can switch shifts with you next week without even asking.

I had a client whom I'll call Pam who wanted to move for a very long time. Pam always saw herself in the country with a bit of land around her. She and her husband, Gary, lived in the city though, and her husband loved the intensity and energy of urban life. Pam, meanwhile, wanted a larger home and to be surrounded by nature. Forty-five minutes from where they currently lived was a much smaller community where you could own land and live more cheaply. Pam often suggested they look into the area, but her husband resisted. She was very sensitive and empathic and he was strong willed and emotionally intense. Pam often let him take the lead on making decisions to keep the peace. After fifteen years of living in the city it was becoming more and more expensive and for this reason Pam's husband became open to considering their options. They looked at communities in the surrounding areas and found a cute one with restaurants and coffee shops and art galleries and very friendly people. They spent a long weekend trying out the area. At the end of it, they were sitting at an outdoor café. Gary turned to Pam and said, "I could see sitting at this café every morning. I'm so happy here. It's a great break from the hustle and bustle of the city. And you know, we're only a short drive away."

When Pam recounted this story for me, she said, "Tanya, I should have been thanking my lucky stars, but instead I was furious. All I kept thinking was that we could have done this ten years ago if I had just pushed a little harder." Gary spoke to his boss and was able to change the time he came and left from the office every day to accommodate his new long commute, and even got Fridays working from home. Their expenses were so much lower in the smaller town that Pam was able to quit her office job and open a shop on Main Street. Since then, Pam has been more vocal about her needs and desires, realizing that sometimes what she wants might be the best thing for both herself and Gary. She was sitting in the back seat instead of co-piloting their life, which wasn't fair to either of them.

Earth angels need to try to negotiate compromises at home and work that are a win for them too. Like telling your child that you will drive them and a friend to the movies and pick them up after if they agree to clean up the kitchen after dinner for two nights. Earth angels may not even be used to looking at situations from the angle of, "Is this a win for me?"

You might work at a company where you have become very attached to your boss. When a position opens up in another department, you might look into applying, only to have your boss say, "Are you sure? I think the position you currently have is better suited to your talents." Or you might have met a new friend you're really excited about. Then one of your close friends says, "I knew someone who went to high school with her, and I think she's someone you should avoid." Who is going to make the decision about what job you apply for or what friends you make? Other people or you? Even if you end up making a mistake or regret your decision, an authentic decision made by you—after taking everyone else's advice onboard—will always be the better choice. Sometimes making the "wrong" choice can be a wonderful way for sensitive people to learn that they are not too fragile and can bounce back from challenging circumstances.

Sensitive Earth Angels Need Space

All sensitive people usually enjoy having a bit of extra space. That's because they pick up on so much. When sensitive folks can come home to a quiet house with calm warm vibes, their own energy can unfurl and relax. This is one reason that some sensitive people may not be itching to live with a romantic partner—they like to be able to control the vibes of their home.

If this idea of having space resonates with you, it does not mean you have to be single or live separately from your partner—although if that is what feels right to you and makes you happy, more power to you. (Living separately all or part of the time is becoming more common among committed couples.)

You might fall in love with someone who is very high energy, extroverted, and expressive. Your love might be bouncing off the walls like a puppy dog, yet you cannot imagine life without this cutie pie. Or you might have some adorable children (human or fur babies) who demand a lot of your attention. Or perhaps you have a roommate you value (or you are living communally with several people). The trick to a sensitive person navigating any relationship is to stay grounded in their own emotional skin and to know the needs of their own system.

If you have a very high energy and expressive partner who likes to be with you a lot (and congrats if you have found someone who realizes how amazing you are), it might be about having time and space to retreat. This need for retreat time is something you can communicate to your partner and eventually will be something they just accept about you, like, "My wife takes her coffee black" or "My husband prefers the color navy blue."

This notion of the sensitive person being able to retreat is key for any romantic relationship you are in. The amount of time and space you need to retreat will certainly be different for each individual. It might be having an hour to unwind when you walk in the door from work, either by taking a walk, getting lost in a creative project, watching a great tv show, prepping dinner, or listening to a podcast on an interesting subject. If you are a parent, it might be about making a deal with your spouse or getting child-care coverage if you are single for a certain amount of retreat time every week so you can go to the basement and meditate or go for a drive in the country or get your hands wonderfully dirty in the garden with no interruptions from little ones. Interruptions when a sensitive person needs alone time are no fun for anyone.

It's key to let loved ones know, which includes children and friends, that the need to retreat has nothing to do with them. Your absence has no reflection on how much you care for them. Letting someone you are dating know that you need a night off or even a weekend off, and explaining to them that this is part of your sensitivity, will help avoid any feelings of rejection or abandonment.

My mother had a routine for us on the weekends. On Saturday afternoons, once we got to a certain age of being physically and mentally self-sufficient, she would tell my brother and I to each go to our rooms and entertain ourselves for a few hours. We could not play together and could not come into her bedroom—the doors to our bedrooms had to be shut. While we had one television in the home, it was kept in the living room. And since this was before laptops, cell phones, and internet, our options were limited about how we spent our time. We could read, or draw … and that was about it. "I want you to get comfortable with being alone," Mom told us. She also told us she looked forward to these hours every week, where she could close her door, put on her classical music and read *The New Yorker*. Was my mom sensitive? Definitely.

The first few times I was in that room alone, which was during my middle school years, I remember being frustrated and confused. What was I supposed to do? I mean I could not watch television and I was not allowed to talk to a friend on the phone. I honed in on music, and soon I was performing the entire Fleetwood Mac *Rumors* album in my bedroom to—no one. Although looking back maybe my guardian angels were clapping and being quite entertained. I had a ball doing it. I would switch up who I was on stage—sometimes I was Stevie Nicks and sometimes I was the drummer Mick Fleetwood, etc.

My mom knew she needed time each week to retreat. She did not have a romantic partner in the house, so she let her roommates (her kids) know instead. If you live with a friend or roommate, gently letting them know that retreat time is important to you can make your cohabitation much more pleasurable and successful. If you are living with a romantic partner or about to move in with one, explaining your sensitivity and the need to occasionally or regularly retreat is about developing even more intimacy with this person as you let them know who you are and what your needs are on a core level. That this retreat time is how you honor your sensitivity, come back home to yourself, and protect your nervous system from overstimulation. Your partner might come back and say, "Well, I need a certain amount of cuddle time every week." As an earth angel, that probably suits you just fine.

Earth Angel Exercise
Finding Healthy Ways to Retreat

Retreat is how the sensitive person gets their nervous system to settle back into neutral. Just reading a positive or engrossing book and listening to gentle music is like giving your nervous system a nap. Make sure romantic partners understand this so retreat time does not become a source of arguments—the opposite of relaxing and very overstimulating.

Below are some suggestions for healthy retreat time. If you feel you are retreating too much because the world feels overwhelming and you are starting to feel more isolated than nourished, ask for help from a loved one or health-care provider. You will notice that the following are all solo activities to give you a break from other people's energy. Rate each of these retreat techniques from one to four, one being indifference and four being "I love this idea." When you are done, count up all the threes and fours and find ways to incorporate them into your life if you haven't already:

1. **Meditate at work:** Take some time out, whether it's five or twenty minutes, to meditate during the day. If you work outside the home and have a door on your office, shut it to meditate. If you work in an open office setting, take a walk on your lunch break and quiet your mind that way. If it's difficult for you to quiet your mind, try meditating while sitting on a park bench and listening to calming music or chanting.

2. **Curl up with a great print book:** As an author and bibliophile, I of course encourage you to read more, though there

is additional value in this very low-stimulation activity. Watching a film or listening to someone talk in a podcast are also relaxing but are more stimulating than simply reading. Reading is great right before bed to help your nervous system quiet down and prepare for a good night's sleep. While I think digital books are an excellent way to help the environment, I also think getting away from a screen is much more relaxing for your nervous system.

3. **Be in a quiet spot in nature.** Your child's little league game may be held in a beautiful park, but it's hardly a low-stimulation environment. Take a walk through a safe park early in the morning or during the day if you work from home when not many people will be around. If you have a backyard or porch that looks out on nature, chilling there for a bit is wonderful retreat time (as long as it's not too noisy—e.g., cars whizzing by or children loudly playing). I have windows in my house that face out onto tall trees, and just gazing out for a minute or two can calm me.

4. **Get lost in a creative project you can do on autopilot.** Have you been knitting so long that your hands simply know what to do without much input from your brain? Or maybe you are a great cook and can whip up a gourmet meal without having to think hard about it. These are examples of how creative projects can be soothing retreat time. If you are on a deadline for a creative project that is earning you money, it may not be as relaxing because of the financial and timing pressure and the need to be fully present during the process.

5. **Exercise solo.** Walking alone or pulling out your yoga mat at home and doing a few simple poses by yourself works

well. Gyms can be a little too overstimulating on days when you are feeling really on edge and the gym is crowded. When you are able, exercising can be a wonderful way to clear your mind and move stuck, stagnant energy out of your field.

6. **Take a shower.** Friends and clients who live with a number of people (e.g., several roommates or a spouse and several children) tell me that the bathroom is one of the few places they can retreat. To be mindful of water consumption, I won't suggest taking a shower for hours, but you might pop in for a quick shower and lather up to help clear your energy and retreat.

7. **Journal about what you're grateful for.** Put on some calming music, light a candle, and write a journal entry. Try writing about something nourishing and not too overstimulating, such as to count your blessings. You might even do this on a day that has been particularly challenging to go back and think about anything positive that happened.

8. **Take some time for yourself while your child naps.** Many parents use nap time as a chance to catch up on other things. Occasionally when it's possible, use this as retreat time. Just having a quiet house invites the nervous system to settle down. Part of retreating is anchoring back into your own energy after being out in the world or wrapped up in other people's energy.

Do Earth Angels Have a Romantic Type?

In general, the answer is no, there is no ideal type of person for an earth angel to be with, though we'll cover some of the people earth angels might be attracted to in a shadow sense, the part of us we are unaware of or do not want to own. Each earth angel has soul contracts to come together with certain lovers to awaken each other, heal, and also simply fall in love and partner. These will obviously be unique to each earth angel; as each earth angel has a unique personality and destiny, the people each earth angel will find attractive will be unique as well.

I think more than a type, earth angels have a romantic requirement—that their partners understand and honor earth angel energy. A successful partnership is about both people really understanding and accepting who the other person is. Of course we can try to teach our partners and help them grow and evolve—no one came to earth *not* to evolve, after all—but there must also be some level of acceptance of who these people are at their core.

If you're an earth angel, being sensitive is part of your core. If someone is a musician at their core, a partner might have to accept that they want to go on tour. Or if they have a straight job, that playing gigs here and there and continuing to grow in their craft is important. Maybe your earth angel-ness lead you to want to be a counselor or be a mother. These are things your partner might not simply have to tolerate but embrace and celebrate.

What does being an earth angel mean to you? How does it manifest in your life now and how would you like it to manifest in the future? When you become clear on these items, you know yourself and can better explain what is fundamental about you to your partner. Leave the door open to change too—what you want today may be very different from what you want five years from now. Couples should get in the habit of talking regularly about how they are each changing and evolving.

Earth angels don't have to partner with another sensitive person. Yet after doing so many readings on sensitive people, I think it really helps if sensitive people partner with others who understand and accept this sensitivity. If you believe your partner doesn't understand right now, give them the chance to do so. Talk to them about the information in this book and any parts that resonated strongly with you.

Earth Angel Exercise
Earth Angels in Love

This short exercise will help get you more in touch with how being an earth angel has affected your current and past relationships. There are no right or wrong answers, only whatever is unique to your experience. This exercise should help you get clear on how your earth angel identity fits into your romantic life. If you are having challenges in a current romantic partnership or are between romantic partners, these questions have the potential to be even more thought-provoking and the answers insightful.

1. Is there something specific about your earth angel-ness that your current partner or your last partner has or had a hard time accepting, honoring, understanding, or celebrating?

2. What aspects of your earth angel-ness have been difficult or caused problems in your romantic life up until now?

3. Have you ever been with a partner who seemed to understand and even celebrate your earth angel-ness?

4. Were you ever with someone romantically who did not understand your sensitivity at first, but then in time came to understand and honor it well?

5. Have you ever been with a partner that always stepped on your sensitivity?

6. Do you feel like your sensitivity sometimes or in some ways holds you back in romance?

7. How has being sensitive helped your romantic life?

8. Have you ever dated anyone else who was very sensitive? Was that a positive, negative, or neutral experience?

9. What do you wish your current partner or last romantic partner would understand or could have understood about your earth angel-ness?

10. Have you ever slipped into codependency and managing someone else's emotions with a partner because of your sensitivity?

11. How do you set healthy boundaries regarding your sensitivity and romantic partners?

12. Looking back on some of your earliest romantic relationships, how was your sensitivity understood by your partners? How was it honored or not honored?

13. Have some of these early relationship experiences set up patterns in your current or recent relationship?

14. How would you like current and future partners to honor you and your sensitivity?

15. How would you explain your earth angel-ness to a partner?

16. What talks about sensitivity have you and your current or potential partner already had? Do you feel they understand the concepts?

17. Is talking about these things difficult, easy, or somewhere in the middle with your current partner or potential future partners? Why?

18. Have you ever been in a romantic relationship with another earth angel?

19. Has reading this book made you change or reevaluate your approach to your current partner or to potential future partners?

20. What information in this book are you most excited to communicate to a partner or try out in a romantic relationship?

21. Are you aware of what a loving, nurturing, valuable partner you are or can be simply because you are a sensitive earth angel?

Earth Angel Shadows and Unhealthy Partnerships

The Jungian model of the shadow refers to anything—positive or negative—that exists outside of our conscious mind. A shadow motivation would be any motivation that exists on a subconscious or unconscious level, one we are not consciously aware of yet is very active in making decisions. When we can get clear on some of our shadow or subconscious motivations, this really helps us shift self-sabotaging patterns that seem to haunt us or "curse" us.

When it comes to romance, earth angels can have shadow loyalties to wounded birds, romantic partners who have a wing that needs mending. We've all got our issues; I'm not advocating waiting until someone is perfect (it'll never happen) or every single issue being worked through before dating. If you are an earth angel who falls in love with a hot mess, more power to you. My husband and I got married fairly young and worked through our issues as they came up in the marriage (there were/are *plenty*) and helped each other grow. Even today, we are still working through our issues together.

It's important to be aware of how much of your attraction to someone else is about them as a person versus how much is about their suffering and your desire to heal or "fix" them. As previously covered, earth angels really enjoy helping people in significant ways and can be attracted to professions that require it of them, but please make sure it's not *only* the earth angel in you attracted to someone else. I think sometimes when earth angels have not found a way to act out their mission in the world, they use their romantic life as an outlet. Several past clients of mine ended up changing their profession to the healing arts, whereupon their love lives suddenly improved dramatically. They were no longer attracted to the dark, wounded romantic partner. They were now able to scratch the healing itch in their careers and did not need to act the impulse out in their love lives. If this resonates with you, it does not mean you have to change your whole career, *but* it might mean you have to look at how you can better live as an earth angel in your life outside of romance.

Some earth angels I've had as clients believed they were in relationships with people who tended to be narcissistic. Whether a product of childhood neglect or a personality tendency, the term "narcissism" itself can be used in a casual or clinical sense, so it might be good to talk to a professional about the matter. Above all, do not become an earth angel who enables narcissism in someone else.

Do you have a pattern of being attracted to people who do not give much to you? Are you always the one in the relationship who does the nurturing? While I think it's natural for earth angels to take on the role of nurturer in a romantic relationship, it's also important for them to feel nurtured back. Nurturing other people when you are an earth angel feels lovely because it's part of your collective mission, just as someone who is meant to be an artist or teacher feels good doing those things. So naturally you might be the type that loves to spoil your mate. Every relationship is unique; there is no formula that will work for every couple. Just make sure that you are not doing all the caretaking, or that all your earth angel energy is going straight to your partner. Save some for yourself—and the rest of the world.

Earth Angel Quiz
Do You Give Too Much?

Take a few deep breaths before you answer the following questions. Know that as an earth angel, you are already prone to giving too much. Please answer these honestly. If you are not in a romantic relationship right now, think about your most recent relationships or how you tend to act in a relationship and answer from that perspective. Read all the categories afterward as you might find that no matter what your score, you relate to aspects of each.

If some answers leave you feeling upset, please know that just because you didn't like your results of this quiz it does *not* mean you need to leave your relationship. It does not mean you are better than your partner or they are a bad person. What it might mean is that you think about this quiz for a bit and then have a loving, honest talk with your partner. Many times if both people are open, the dynamics of a relationship can change for the better. Just because you have a certain pattern romantically does not mean you must keep repeating this pattern in the future.

Answer the following with A for almost always, B for sometimes, and C for hardly ever.

1. Do you often anticipate the needs of your partner before the need even arises? Like bringing them some fresh water or a snack before they even realize they are thirsty or hungry,

or suggesting they take a break from their work before they even realize they are tired?

2. Does your partner say things like, "My partner takes such good care of me," to other people?

3. Do you often have your challenging emotional experiences alone? Like if you are very disappointed by a situation or just feeling depressed about your circumstances, do you tend not to share because you don't want to upset your partner?

4. Do you emotionally hold your partner's hand through their challenging experiences? Are you their rock or their "therapist"?

5. Do you find that you don't always voice your needs in the relationship, even though your partner is vocal about their needs?

6. Do you often look back and say, "I wish I would have spoken up for myself there" or "I wish I would have pushed for us to make a different decision as a couple that time"?

7. Do you get great pleasure from pampering your partner, yet you don't get a lot of pampering in return?

8. Does your partner call the shots or make the majority of important practical decisions like where you live, who you socialize with as a couple, etc.?

9. Do you find yourself often deferring to what your partner wants, like where they would like to eat or what they want to do on a Saturday afternoon?

10. When you do stand up for what you want, is there a sort of rebellion from your partner?

11. Do you often rub your partner's back or feet, yet they rarely do this for you?

12. Does your partner find it easy to ask for what they want in the bedroom, yet you find it difficult?

13. Is your partner's time (like the time they spend at work or on a hobby or with their friends) considered sacred in the house, yet your time is considered flexible and up for grabs?

14. Are mealtimes and bedtimes things that revolve around what is best for your partner's schedule?

15. Do you feel bad about making a purchase for yourself when the financial situation is comfortable?

16. When you are considering the happiness of the household, is it usually your partner's happiness you are considering?

17. Do you find yourself biting your lip about your partner's bad behavior or habits, or just "living with it," when you would like to speak up or your instincts are to do so?

18. Has your partner asked you to give up something very important and fundamental to you, or have you given up something very important and fundamental to you without a fight?

Mostly As—An earth angel who may be giving too much

You are probably a natural nurturer and a sensitive earth angel who can really pick up on other people's emotions. You might be trying to manage your partner's emotional experience by sometimes denying your own. Speaking up for yourself, and feeling safe and supported as you do, is key. You might concentrate on your throat chakra, the energy center that manages our ability to speak up for what we want and need. Tune in to this energy center in your throat. Does it seem blocked? If so, how much? Forty percent? More than that? As you tune in to your throat chakra with your feelers, your throat might actually feel tight for a few seconds if that particular chakra is blocked. Practice speaking up more about what you need and want, whether it's asking your partner to help out around the house or pursuing a dream of yours. Ask yourself if you learned not to speak up in childhood or an early romantic partner trained you not to speak up. Sometimes not speaking up comes from fear or learned experience that our needs won't be met even if we do speak up. Finding out where our patterns come from is key to changing them. You care deeply about other people, which is one of your greatest gifts and strengths. Look for more balance regarding how much you give others and get support from a counselor if you need it.

Mostly Bs—An earth angel who is discovering balance

You probably like giving and are in touch with the fact that nurturing others and supporting them gives you pleasure. Yet you know that sometimes you have to practice healthy selfishness. There might be times when you look back on decisions made as a couple and think, "I wish I had fought harder (or at all) for what I wanted." It could be helpful to have a way to hold yourself accountable as an earth angel, like journal occasionally about what you feel are your current needs and desires and feel into how often those are being met. Your emotions should be a good barometer of if you are in healthy earth angel mode or over-giving, submissive mode. Recognize what it feels like when you are exhausted and resentful from over-giving and how not speaking up for yourself actually feels uncomfortable and anxiety-producing in the moment. Also notice how it feels to be well taken care of and supported, by yourself and others. It seems from your answers you are good at asking for your own needs to be met and saying no with love while still being a supportive, nurturing earth angel to others.

Mostly Cs—An earth angel who has strong boundaries

Congratulations on having such strong boundaries. This might be something you've always had, or something you had to work very hard at after having weak or no boundaries. Did you see a parent who modeled good boundaries for you to learn from? Or perhaps they gave too much and often felt used up or neglected, and you said to yourself, "That will never be me!" Maybe you had a relationship where you felt you were taken advantage of and learned a difficult but priceless lesson, or you might have experienced a partner who treated you exceptionally well. Remind yourself that it's okay to catch yourself sometimes giving too much—after all, you are an earth angel who loves to give. You have strong enough boundaries that you will quickly catch yourself and recalibrate. It's also okay to question your boundaries occasionally and redraw them. You might decide you need to be more flexible with your boundaries when someone is really hurting or challenged. Feeling free to nurture and being nurtured in return is what love means to an earth angel like you.

Earth Angels, Codependency, and Healthy Detachment

We have already talked a bit about codependency—feeling like the needs of another are more important than your own, or that you cannot feel okay until someone else feels okay first—which I think sensitive people can be more prone to. This is because of the sensitive person's ability to pick up on and even merge with another person's emotions and energy. Yet other people's emotions are not your jurisdiction and not your issue to resolve. This can be a tough lesson for earth angels to learn because they are not only sensitive but possess a strong impulse to help others.

There are some signs of codependency earth angels might watch for in romantic relationships or close relationships with loved ones, including people like children or best friends. Have you ever felt it absolutely intolerable to know that someone you love is upset with you? Has a fight with a best friend that your logical mind tells you will blow over left you feeling pure panic? In this situation, it is your *friend's* opinion of you that dictates your sense of safety and well-being. It's normal and even healthy to fight with friends and lovers, but when we are codependently attached to someone, a fight that others would put into perspective instead feels like the end of the world.

If someone you love is upset and hurting, can you empathize with them, send out a little prayer, let them know you are here for whatever they need, and then go back into your own emotional experience of life? Or do you feel like you will never be able to feel at peace while this loved one is hurting or their situation is unresolved?

Sensitive earth angels must guard against letting someone else's experience control their own experience or sense of well-being. It's perhaps an easy scenario to slip into when you are empathic and care for someone very much. Yet merging with another this way—whether they are a client, boss, or anyone you interact with intimately—tears away at the protective layer guarding your own emotional skin and can leave you feeling raw. You might feel absolutely lost if this person begins to distance themselves from you or is upset with you. The healthy sense of being separate from others is lost, and your own needs get lost too.

The dangers of codependence may be one that earth angels have to learn the hard way. Can you think back to anyone in your life whom you have empathically merged with, probably unconsciously, and then their exiting your life felt absolutely devastating? Is there a face or name that immediately comes to mind? It might have felt like they took a little piece of you with them. While merging with others might seem very seductive to a sensitive earth angel especially in romance, it can create a codependent bond that is self-sabotaging.

Practice creating healthy boundaries with loved ones. Hang up the phone after a friend tells you about their challenges and focus your attention elsewhere to something in *your* life or something uplifting. Practice staying emotionally centered when someone you love gets angry at you, reminding yourself that it is not the end of the world. If you have trouble focusing on others more than yourself, ask yourself if you are doing this to avoid problems in your own life. Sometimes we get caught up in other people's drama as a convenient way of distracting from our own. Realize when you are playing out old childhood drama with people, like being clingy with a lover or a boss because your mother was absent from your childhood life or was distant.

You may find that life sends you some perfect ways to practice healthy detachment. Sometimes we learn a lesson only by doing the exact opposite. Above all, notice how practicing healthy detachment with the people you love actually helps you be a calmer, happier, more balanced version of you, and a better earth angel to the people you care about.

Healthy detachment helps you stay grounded and give loved ones good advice. When you are calm, your intuition is not blocked by strong emotions. If your loved one is experiencing a storm, be the breakwater that their emotional intensity can crash against and then recede. If you go on the emotional, topsy-turvy voyage with them, it will likely do neither of you any good. If you feel codependency is a real issue for you, get support.

Sensitive and Earth Angel Children

You might have a sensitive earth angel child in your family who is very concerned about the feelings of others. They might start an anti-bullying campaign at their school or befriend another child who is often left out socially. Encourage sensitive earth angel children to honor their instinct to nurture themselves and others, while also helping them accept that life isn't fair, and that pain and suffering are a part of the earthly experience.

Sensitive children can so sense and be affected by the emotions of others that they worry they have done something wrong if others are upset or offer to do something to help as if they alone could change their parents' mood. This can be the ideal time to teach them, very young, that just because they can easily sense another person's mood, it does not mean they are responsible for someone else's mood.

If there's a sensitive child in your life, whether it's your own child, a grandchild, a student you teach, a neighbor you play with, or your niece or nephew, take a moment and connect with yourself at that age. As an adult earth angel, what do you most wish a sensitive adult would have taught you about sensitivity? We all develop coping skills in childhood that, for better and worse, are often carried with us into adulthood as default responses. Help a sensitive child in your life learn to manage their emotions and sensitivity so it will be easier for them to do the same when they are older. Simply helping sensitive children understand, manage, and navigate overstimulation would be an amazing present, one that would last a child's entire life. There is so much information out there on sensitive children that if you have one in your life, don't be afraid to research and learn more. Always check with a child's parent or guardian *before* sharing new concepts with the child.

Earth Angels Make Excellent Friends, Family Members, and Romantic Partners

I wanted to end this chapter with a reminder that as an earth angel, you have qualities that will always be highly valued by others. Earth angels make loyal, devoted friends, lovers, and family members. I'm lucky enough to have some in my life. Earth angels can be such a comfort and often act as a soft landing place for those around them. Whenever you are looking to bring new people into your personal life, have confidence that as a tender-hearted earth angel you have so much to offer another human in a relationship of any kind.

Developing relationships with other sensitive earth angels, no matter what role they play to you, can be very healing. These people might feel safe or being around them might feel like you've come home. If you would like to bring more sensitive earth angels into your life, ask your divine angels to send some your way or help you better recognize sensitive earth angels in your environment. You can also look into groups of sensitive earth angels who meet regularly, perhaps in the guise of a book club, volunteer group, or spiritual community.

You might spend a moment now reflecting on all the earth angels who have touched your life as friends, teachers, or health-care providers. It won't be hard to bring this kind of person to mind, because that loving, supportive energy always stands out—and yours does too.

Conclusion
An Earth Angel Named Loraine

As I was nearing the end of my journey writing this book, the question of how I would conclude it loomed. I knew I wanted to inspire earth angels to honor their personal needs and desires, live their earth angel mission of compassion and service, and practice great self-care to protect and hone their special sensitivity. It struck me that I could do this by somehow reminding earth angels how precious and important their earthly experience is, having come here as souls to try to live with great presence, purpose, and meaning.

Then one day I was sitting in a favorite writing spot, on my porch, listening to the birds and looking out at the trees and feeling very content. Suddenly, I saw a face in my mind—Loraine, an earth angel I'd known briefly and deeply admired.

If you knew Loraine, you could easily picture her smile, just as I did. She was *always* smiling. Loraine possessed a strong, ebullient energy, and as an earth angel I think she understood the subtle yet profound power of energy and how hers could positively affect others.

Loraine was a smart, wise, funny lady. She was nobody's fool, yet her manner was as open as someone you might mistake for being naïve. This was really her natural earth angel optimism, or a natural tendency to look on the bright side. When symptoms Loraine assumed were exhaustion turned out to be signs of advanced cancer, she changed her life and devoted herself to healing. She trained as a nutritionist, fought cancer for years, and posted about health on her social media, a way to give her struggle meaning as she used it to encourage and educate others. Whether it was a snap of a colorful salad bowl with a technical description of exactly why every ingredient was good for you, or a picture of her wiry warrior frame fist pumping after she had been given the all-clear by her doctors, she shared the ups and downs of her healing journey with a courageous honesty that truly inspired others. Creating meaning and inspiration—as well as comfort—for others are things earth angels are exceptionally good at.

When I first learned Loraine had died, it felt impossible. How could someone so alive pass away? Loraine delighted in even the smallest details of daily life, like finding a great purse on sale or taking a swim at the local YMCA. Taking the small details of daily life others might view as insignificant and celebrating them is something earth angels have a large innate capacity for. Loraine also had a healthy sense of humor, something earth angels need to sustain their spirits and help take the edge off the challenges and disappointments of their earthly journey.

My strongest memory of Loraine was sitting at a restaurant where a bunch of people were meeting for after-work drinks. Some were talking about former colleagues they all had in common and blowing off steam by complaining about their quirks. The complaints were in a spirit of levity, but I remember glancing at Loraine and seeing how agitated she suddenly became. Teasing other people when they weren't there to defend themselves was something she just wasn't comfortable with. Loraine said nothing, but after a few minutes she made an excuse and left. As an earth angel, she was very concerned with what felt fair and ethical, even in casual situations.

After Loraine left this life, I connected with a mutual friend who also knew Loraine and we reminisced about this special earth angel. "When I first met Loraine we instantly clicked," my friend said. "I can't explain it. Loraine just had that *lightness* to her. Always sunny, happy, and kind." Not every earth angel is always sunny, happy, and kind (Spirit knows I'm not), especially if they are experiencing burnout. For Loraine, it seemed as though approaching life with hope and compassion was her default mode, though I'm sure Loraine had moments that weren't so light, like all earth angels. As I said before, it is important to honor, process, and express emotions—especially the challenging, negative, or messy ones. Like many earth angels, Loraine had the gift of presence—the ability to give her full attention to someone and make them feel important and cared for, whether she had known them five years or five minutes. She was the kind of person who started affectionately referring to you as "hon," "babe," or "girl" as soon as she met you.

When I searched the internet about Loraine after her passing, I only found a couple of things: some lovely pictures—she was stunningly beautiful, though it's just as likely that it was her magnetic earth angel energy shining through—and touching messages on the web from friends after her death. Looking for Loraine's digital footprint was a reminder that being an earth angel isn't necessarily a destiny that will make you famous; many earth angels live remarkable lives of touching others, yet go down in history as unsung heroes. However, the people who knew them personally will never forget. There's just something about an earth angel like Loraine that stays with you and leaves an imprint on your heart.

Your time on earth is precious, my angel. I hope this book helps you enjoy it even more and use your earthly time well.

Appendix

Angel Playlist

Looking for some angelic inspiration? Make a playlist from the angel-themed songs below. Listening to music about angels can get you more in touch with your inner earth angel and bring you closer to your divine angels. When you hear a song that mentions angels, take note and add it to your playlist.

"Angel" by Madonna

"Soldier's Angel" by Stevie Nicks

"There Must Be an Angel (Playing with My Heart)" by Eurythmics

"Little Wing" by Jimi Hendrix

"Angel Flying Too Close to the Ground" by Willie Nelson

"She Talks to Angels" by the Black Crowes

"Angel" by Aerosmith

"Angel of Harlem" by U2

"Calling All Angels" by k.d. lang and Jane Siberry

"Angel Band" by Emmylou Harris

"Angel" by Sinead O'Connor

"Through the Eyes of an Angel" by Deva Premal and Miten

"Angel" by Enya

"Angels Cry" by Mariah Carey

"Angels Among Us" by Alabama

"Angel from Montgomery" by Bonnie Raitt and John Prine

"Fly to the Angels" by Slaughter

"Angel Eyes" by Jeff Healey

"Angel" by Elvis

"She Gave Her Angels" by Prince

"Angel" by Aretha Franklin

"Golden Years" by David Bowie

"Waiting on an Angel" by Ben Harper

"In the Arms of an Angel" by Sarah McLachlan

"Everybody's Got an Angel" by Cyndi Lauper

"Send Me an Angel" by Scorpions

"Angels" by Robbie Williams

"Angel of the Morning" by Juice Newton

"Angel" by Shaggy

"Concrete Angel" by Martina McBride

"Calling All Angels" by Train

"Angel's Song" by Chloe Agnew

"Send Me an Angel" by Real Life

"When You Come Back Down" by Nickel Creek

Recommended Reading

Aron, Elaine N. *The Highly Sensitive Person: How to Thrive When the World Overwhelms You.* New York: Broadway Books, 1997.

Cain, Susan. *Quiet: The Power of Introverts in a World That Can't Stop Talking.* New York: Broadway Books, 2013.

Choquette, Sonia. *Walking Home: A Pilgrimage from Humbled to Healed.* Carlsbad, CA: Hay House, 2014.

Dyer, Wayne. *Getting in the Gap: Making Conscious Contact with God Through Meditation.* Carlsbad, CA: Hay House, 2014.

Frankl, Viktor. *Man's Search for Meaning.* Boston, MA: Beacon Press, 1946.

Loewe, Emma, and Lindsay Kellner. *Spirit Almanac: A Modern Guide to Ancient Self-Care*. New York: Tarcher Perigee, 2018.

Orloff, Judith. *The Empath's Survival Guide: Life Strategies for Sensitive People*. Boulder, CO: Sounds True, 2017.

Richardson, Cheryl. *The Art of Extreme Self-Care: Transform Your Life One Month at a Time*. Carlsbad, CA: Hay House, 2012.

Richardson, Tanya Carroll. *Angel Insights: Inspiring Messages From and Ways to Connect With Your Spiritual Guardians*. Woodbury, MN: Llewellyn, 2016.

———. *Angel Intuition: A Psychic's Guide to the Language of Angels*. Woodbury, MN: Llewellyn, 2018.

———. *Forever in My Heart: A Grief Journal*. Berkeley, CA: Ulysses Press, 2016.

———. *Zen Teen: 40 Ways to Stay Calm When Life Gets Stressful*. Berkeley, CA: Seal Press, 2018.

Sherman, Paulette Kouffman. *Sacred Baths: 52 Bathing Rituals to Revitalize Your Spirit*. Woodbury, MN: Llewellyn, 2016.

Silver, Tosha. *It's Not Your Money: How to Live Fully from Divine Abundance*. Carlsbad, CA: Hay House, 2019.

Tessler, Bari. *The Art of Money: A Life-Changing Guide to Financial Happiness*. Berkeley, CA: Parallax Press, 2016.

Tolle, Eckhart. *The Power of Now: A Guide to Spiritual Enlightenment*. Vancouver, BC: Namaste Publishing, 2004.

Valentine, Radleigh. *How to Be Your Own Genie: Manifesting the Magical Life You Were Born to Live*. Carlsbad, CA: Hay House, 2017.

Whitehurst, Tess. *Unicorn Magic: Awaken to Mystical Energy & Embrace Your Personal Power*. Woodbury, MN: Llewellyn, 2019.

Wix, Angela. *Llewellyn's Little Book of Unicorns*. Woodbury, MN: Llewellyn, 2019.